Christmas Letters FROM HELL

ALL THE NEWS WE HATE FROM THE PEOPLE WE LOVE

MICHAEL LENT

A FIRESIDE BOOK
Published by Simon & Schuster
New York London Toronto Sydney

FIRESIDE
A Division of Simon & Schuster, Inc.
1230 Avenue of the Americas
New York, NY 10020

First Fireside trade paperback edition November 2007

FIRESIDE and colophon are registered trademarks
of Simon & Schuster, Inc.

For information about special discounts for bulk purchases,
please contact Simon & Schuster Special Sales at 1-800-456-6798
or business@simonandschuster.com.

Designed by Jill Weber

Manufactured in the United States of America

10 9 8 7 6 5 4 3 2 1

Library of Congress Cataloging-in-Publication Data
Lent, Michael.
Christmas letters from hell: all the news we hate from the people we
love / Michael Lent.
p. cm
1. Christmas—Humor. 2. Letters—Humor. I. Title.
PN6231.C36L46 2007
816'.6—dc22   2007019429

ISBN-13: 978-1-4165-3996-4
ISBN-10:   1-4165-3996-4

Dedicated to Willem and Sophia

INTERACTIVE FEATURE!

LICK THIS PAGE

TO REVEAL A

SECRET MESSAGE

FROM THE AUTHOR!

Introduction

'Tis the season to put aside petty differences, like restraining orders and outstanding warrants, in favor of the time-honored tradition of sending and receiving Christmas letters that truly reflect the spirit of the season.

Spanning the generations, it's easy to imagine our founding fathers taking time to pen a report on the accomplishments of, say, their livestock, with a *Jefferson Family News Roundup*. Certainly, what better way than amateur journalism to chronicle in detail the big summer vacation RV excursion through thirty-eight states, who in the extended family has taken up tap dancing, got that all-important promotion to waste-treatment-plant supervisor, or is heroically battling a bladder condition?

More than just a braggarts' trip to bountiful, where even middle schoolers are touched by greatness at the science fair, only Christmas letters can serve readers a steaming, savory holiday blend of family news, holiday cheer, stretched truth, and alleged humor that can depict all of the pulse-pounding excitement of day-to-day life in North Dakota, or the indomitable spirit of a distant relative's neighbor who recently conquered shingles. These Yuletide epistles ask us to look deep within ourselves, and take inventory of our lives. Often, the result is some boldly crafted, hard-charging, if highly fictitious, alter egos printed on red or green paper.

What follows is a collection of the best of the best collection of do-gooders and go-getters of the past, present, and future. So, sit back, relax, and ask yourself, "What if my Christmas tree were home to killer bees?" or "What if dear old Saint Nick presided over a multinational corporation?" or "What if bin Laden had been a high-school exchange student in Minnesota?" or "I wonder what Global Warming has been up to?" Indeed, "What if Thoreau wrote a holiday blog from Walden Pond?" or "What if a child's letter to Santa crossed paths with that of a Nigerian scam artist?" And, while you're at it, "What if the family dog used the Christmas letter as a platform to discuss his recent neutering?" And, of course, "What if Satan kept everyone abreast of his latest goings-on?"

I'm not saying none of these events actually happened, although the killer-bee scenario grows ever more likely. No one can say for sure. I'm just saying, "What if?"

Merry Chrisnukwanzaakah!

Christmas Letters
FROM
HELL

Letter from Santa

ANNUAL REPORT TO SHARE HOLDERS

MANY OF YOU HAVE WRITTEN to express consternation following the most recent INS raid on the North Pole. You small children should not fret so at seeing Rudolph on the evening news, being tazered and put in a squad car. Believe you me and Mrs. Claus, if it were possible to find American elves still willing to work for snowflakes and gumdrops, well, we most certainly would have looked into it by now. After the recent quintuple bypass on Santa's ol' ticker (the cargo containers of sugar cookies I received were a wonderful if ironic gesture), I certainly don't have time or the heart to clean the reindeer stables, shovel snow, de-ice walkways, or make those wonderful snow angels by hand that are especially H-E-double-L on old Santa's sciatica. Valued friends like Jorge, Ernesto, Lupe, and my personal favorite, Manny, did lots to ease Santa's burden and were truly almost like family. We are sorry indeed to see them heading back to Ecuador. Not to worry, Santa is still on the job—it takes more than bureaucratic bah humbug to spoil the Christmas spirit.

Effective immediately, we will be outsourcing production to the Yan Yuanzhang Ming Twang Province of China. By jiggers, that's a mouthful! As you'll soon see, on the fanciful candy cane flowchart I'll be leaving under your yuletide tree, the cost-benefit advantage is manifold. By gosh, for one thing, China keeps its currency, the yuan, fixed at a set rate against the dollar, and undervalued by as much as 40 percent. That's sure good news for manufacturers like us, who can produce goods like those toys you love so inexpensively in China and ship them on time via the new global leader in shipping, Polemerica Industries. ("Trust the bearded men in red and white for all your packing needs and you'll go ho-ho-ho!")

Gosh golly, some of this news is bound to upset the tummies of those of you used to the way we did things in those bygone days. It sure took Ol' Santa some adjusting, too. Sadly, intense competition from megaretailers like Store-Mart and Bullseye of Bargains forced us to consider cold, hard, miserly realities of the global marketplace. Following the IPO of 2005, the acquisition of the Foot Bond Medicated Powder Company and subsequent merger with Hyundai in 2006, and the restructuring in the second quarter (Donner has decided to devote more time to family and we sure wish him well in his future endeavors), we're tickled to report that the North Pole is no longer a humble private enterprise solely devoted to bringing smiles to children around the world. (Santa says to tell Mom and Dad to please consider the newly formed subsidiary Polecare for all their pharmaceutical and health insurance needs!) By gosh, it doesn't take an abominable snowman to realize that, by outsourcing to China, we can anticipate substantial projected operating cost reductions of 30 percent over previous per unit expenditures. Further, we anticipate improved or equivalent product quality substantial reduction in operating costs.

As I told you wee ones, these changes may take a bit of getting used to. But, rest assured, even if the name's a little different, we're still the same North Pole you grew up with—although, beginning next quarter, the North Pole will be referred to as the People's Republic of China Manufacturing and Processing Center of Yan Yuanzhang Ming Twang Province and elves shall be called Workers of the People's Manufacturing Collective.

That should bring us up to speed. Ho ho ho!

MERRY CHRISTMAS, EVERYBODY!

*<I;-)

YOUR FRIEND,

Santa Claus

H☀LIDAY
Attack Ad

THEY SAY YOU'RE SUPPOSED to love everyone this holiday season, but here are some things you might not know about Grandma and Grandpa Jenkins.

Grandpa Jenkins claims to love feeding squirrels in the park. But, look closely, and you'll discover what he actually loves is napping on a park bench, then eating the peanuts himself on the walk home.

And what about Grandma Jenkins? She promises you home-baked cookies in the shape of Christmas trees and snowmen, but take a second look. Grandma Jenkins makes just one batch of cookies, then mixes them in with store-bought. Who does she think she's fooling?

What about the time you fell and skinned your knee? Grandma Jenkins kissed the boo-boo and promised to make it better. But it wasn't, was it? You had to apply antiseptic for three whole days.

Grandpa Jenkins says he's a good listener, but he wears two hearing aids and can't hear the difference between Ds, Ps, and Ts. And, even more disturbing, he says he'll see every pass and punt of your Pee Wee

Football season but, with that prostate of his, well, you can be sure of more empty promises while he's "going long."

What about their dog, Jingles? They claim he goes to the groomers every Friday, but who's kidding who? He still looks like a Rastafarian and smells like wet cheese.

Empty words, broken promises, a stinky Rastafarian dog, and store-bought cookies? It's a combination we can't afford to trust.

The choice is clear. This December, let the Jenkins know that enough is enough. Tell your parents you vote to have Christmas with Grandma and Grandpa Lewis in Florida. We have shuffleboard and Nintendo and we bake our own cookies. And our cat La-La is odor free. We promise.

I'M GRANDMA LEWIS and
I APPROVE THIS MESSAGE.

PAID FOR BY THE COALITION FOR A BETTER CHRISTMAS IN FLORIDA

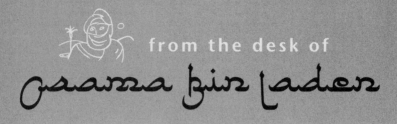

GREETINGS, FAMILY BORNSKY!

I WAS SO DISAPPOINTED TO HEAR that the smoking pipe I sent you arrived broken. It was hand-carved from the skull of a jackal. You are so right, I should have got insurance. Believe me, post offices are all the same. It doesn't matter whether you are in Clump Falls, Minnesota or Kabul. The service is terrible! It makes you want to stone someone to death. I am ranting here.

How is my favorite host family? Can you believe fifteen years has past since I spent my junior year abroad with you for the Radical Muslims in Your Home exchange program? I still have my band uniform around here someplace. Who made the best ambrosia at the Just Say No mixer? Mrs. Bornsky, you did!

Seriously, it feels to me like forever since we sat together in your beautiful den partaking of the Pringles and sharing a good laugh from those *Designing Women*. Seriously, was that one black fellow homosexual or what? One cannot be three feet from Delta Burke and not want at least one taste. It is only my opinion.

I am glad you received my most recent photo. Yes, it is true—I *have* lost weight and not from this South Beach Diet or the Jenny Craig of which you speak. The Clump Falls Beavers football team may have lost an exchange student third-string

linebacker, but the basketball ones have gained a third-string forward who can be dangerous on the perimeter and also for the low post. I don't know what is the low carbs? Actually, forced marches at altitude ten thousand feet are great cardio, my friends. (We can make the Oprah Club for sure with this diet-book winner! Am I right, my friends?)

Tell Steve, he has the styling of the beard and hair issues himself. I can take a joke about mine as well as the next militant, but it is impossible I tell you to find a Fantastic Sams or Supercuts here. So, Steve will be lucky if I do not declare the fatwa on him.

Seriously, what is that guy's problem?

Are those truly ear piercings on little Becky? What happened to the burka I sent last year? Please tell her that, while I appreciated reading her poems "O Pregnant Sky!" And "Middle Finger, Mine!," who, Praise Allah, taught her to read and write? Perhaps I am being too much the doting uncle, but if she is not careful I fear someone will pluck out her eyes and cut off her hands. Then where will her prospects for marriage to the Village Elder be? Seriously, what is going on with kids today?

My current living place is not really suitable for entertaining, so I have not had a true home-warming party as you so wisely suggested. My last residence you would have loved. I should have invited you there when I had the chance. That one-room mud hut was a palace! So much better than the undisclosed location of this drafty cave, high in the remote Pakistani border. Much sadly, American bombs leveled my palatial hut. I ran out into the snow shouting, "Stop! Stop! It's me!" They didn't listen. I found pieces of the welcome mat you sent me in 1999 two miles away. They went too far. Don't get me started on the rant.

Not to be a downer guy, but I must be honest that it just doesn't feel like Christmas to me. I think I have lost the holiday spirit, and not just because I incinerated my beloved collection of American presidents tree ornaments with what I believed was an aroma-therapy candle but was, sadly, in fact a pipe bomb left over from last week's casual explosives Friday.

"Are you ready for the Christmas?" people will ask, and I smile, but deep inside I am at a loss to the answer. A Jewish friend, who I once tried to kill, told me that she has learned to respond with a cheerful "Why, yes, I am!" It is not completely fallacy, because she is as ready any day in December as she was in June. I sense that people do not really want to know if you are ready, they simply want to exclaim about how they are not.

Still, I am determined to decorate this place for the holiday season even if it is only, "Everybody stop by. I have cold cuts for dinner," like Mrs. B used to say.

Actually, the dinner will consist of cold goat-head sandwiches with a gravy I made from my own socks. Talk about the comfort food! Mrs. B, you must surely think that I am giving you a run for your RPGs in the kitchen department! Hah!

Well, I have to go ambush some guys with a carefully prepared rocket attack, so I will close here. Whenever this letter reaches you, rest assured my thoughts will be back in Clump Falls celebrating the *Hammer Time Merry Christmas Special* on the CBS.

And, of course, as always, "Death to the Infidels!" *-)

YOUR PARTNER IN CRIME,

Rizzy

Unseasonable Greetings

FROM YOUR FRIEND, GLOBAL WARMING

A FEW CHRISTMAS HOLIDAYS WITH PEOPLE walking around North Dakota in thongs, and you start talking about me behind my back. Don't try to deny it. Believe me, I've heard the jokes. "Bad news: Florida will be under water. Good news: So will New Jersey," or "Folks in Kansas will finally be able to buy oceanfront property." Laugh it up—enjoy your balmy days while you can. Snow on Christmas morning may be a no-show now, but I was here for the last ice age and, let me tell you, it sure wasn't pretty. Climate change is no joking matter. No, sirree, Bob. Pretty soon you'll say, "It's hot as hell" and it won't be hyperbole, it'll be an AccuWeather forecast.

We've had some fun these past twelve months, haven't we? Who could forget spring break in Utica, New York . . . or the outrageous *bon voyage* party in Vegas for the polar ice-caps? Can you believe we actually ran out of party ice? The irony was hilarious. But I guess that no year in review would be complete without including enough hurricanes and floods to ruin many of your beach vacations. Even in these days of SPF 210, it's hard to tan in a 130 mile per hour wind. Some have accused me of partisan politics, of turning the planet into one giant wet spot just to make Republicans look bad, simply because they want to drive Hummers the size of Cleveland. I say that's nonsense. I mean, how would you like it if your future hung in the balance and depended on Ed Begley, Jr. and Al Gore? Talk about an inconvenient truth! But speaking of greenhouse gases and irreversible thawing, you should check out my new collection of GloWa designer swimwear. It's hot!

I know many of you are saying, "What did polar bears or the environment ever do for me? You go to the Bronx Zoo, and all they do is mope around in their enclosures. If they're so tough, why are they going extinct? And why haven't they logged time ultimate fighting in the Octagon? And that environment is nice and all, especially on a sunny day, but you sure as heck can't eat it." You raise valid points, indeed, just not from where I'm standing. I know some of you have proposed giant wind machines to blow all the bad air to Mexico. Admittedly, I don't have a degree from Cal Tech or MIT, but I'm pretty sure that won't work.

The rumors you've read on the Internet are true: Multinational corporations *are* banking on the earth's demise. For example, both Sizzler and Old Country Buffet are crossbreeding people with manatees and other endangered species to increase their appetites. Judging by the lumbering backsides I see in the Make a Sundae or Fill Your Pockets with Pudding lines I say, "Long live the race of elephant-manatee people!"

For the coming new year, I have just one wish: May you continue to party like it's 1999. That way, the planet and I can finally get some much-needed rest, until a million years from now when the next regime of hyperintelligent bacteria arrives.

But, for now, I wish you all the best and, as the song goes, "I'll stop the world and melt with you."

Warmest Unseasonable Regards,

Your Friend,

Global Warming

Merry Christmas from the Wac-a-Moles

WE SURE MISS CONEY ISLAND, but we want everyone to know that we're doing just fine since our surprise relocation to Fallujah World Theme Park in California. I guess sometimes it takes a whack on the head to appreciate just how random this ol' universe is. The last twelve months after the move started slow enough, but seemed to speed by before we knew it! But who's keeping score? Of course the year wasn't all fun and games—we've had our ups and downs, too. In May, grandpa nearly drowned when someone dumped a Big Gulp down his hole and fried his circuitry. He was offline for quite a while, but we're hoping he will pop up again. The perpetrator got away, but we remain on the lookout. Why is there so much violence in the universe? Anyway, we could never afford a cabinet this nice if we lived out on the prairie. As dad always reminds us, "It's a living," so we should count our blessings. That became painfully clear last May when our one and only mallet was stolen, and someone put a tarp over us for a week. It was depressing, and I longed for the even the most mundane, to-

ken sounds. Before we knew it, it was back to the grindstone.

Cousin Gary is collecting workers' comp, suffering from a repetitive stress injury, and sends his love. He doesn't pop in as much as he used to. These days, Gary spends his time studying genealogy, trying to prove how we are related to Kevin Bacon and Gus the gopher in *Caddy Shack*.

Laney has been making goo-goo eyes at yet another mole from the wrong side of the arcade (for all of you who wonder what happened to Leonard and Bob before that, let's just say, "Who's keeping score, right?"). How many stuffed animal prizes does it take before she learns her lesson about the bad-mole types who duck responsibility?

It's not all gloom in June. As grandma used to say, "It's not whether you win or lose, but how you survive the game." Somebody in high places must have noticed, because we are excited to report that Fox plans a network reality series based on our lives! "Who Wants To Be A Wac-a-Mole" premieres in March. We hope you'll tune in!

To all of our friends in Wisconsin we say,
"Go, Badgers!"

LOVE TO ALL.
YOUR FRIENDS,

The Wac-a-Moles

The Blanc Family 🐾 Holiday Letter 🌲

THIS HOLIDAY SEASON, Mr. Pooders has requested the dubious honor of writing the *Blanc Family Holiday Letter*. Lucky for us, I happened to be in the correct vodka-induced frame of mind when he was kind enough to dictate to me his good wishes and musings. (Please indulge this frustrated Shakespeare trapped in a pooch's body.)

SINCERELY,

Larry Blanc

Dateline December.

My oh my! A new year already upon us? Where did the last seven dog years go? Certainly, this has been my most productive period to date. If there are three rites of passage for a pup: the first licking of the privates; the first territorial marking on the family's antique Persian rug; and, of course, the first time bite of a postal employee's ass, I am now three for three.

As you will notice from the enclosed photo, I have won my battle with that scourge of our generation, mange. At least for now. Why more isn't being done to combat this disease, I do not know. I urge you to bite your congressman. *-)

I must share with you sad news about the untimely passing of my best friend, Rolo, who perhaps unwisely ingested an entire package of Viagra carelessly left unattended on a night stand. Suffice it to say, Rolo went out swinging and there are plenty of lampposts and neighborhood bitches who will long tremble at the thought of those last fourteen hours when Rolo had his way with anything vertical within a five-mile radius. He had a *joie de vivre* admired by all of us who have not been fixed.

December brings snow and ice between one's paws. (I just thought that one up.) It's truly a month requiring more than the usual fourteen hours of sleep for contemplating cosmic questions like, "Why are we here?" and "Why must we be vexed by cats?"

Following Rolo's passing, I have been meditating in my sleep a lot lately. That's helped me forgive my master, Larry.

Speaking of the ball dropping, it's safe to say that I haven't been the same canine since the neutering incident. It's certainly a paradox of life that no matter how many balls one fetches, none of them will ever be your own.

My meditations have also helped me deal with having a cat as a neighbor. After all, is it not true that all is clouded by desire? Where I once barked out of outrage and anger, now I merely lick with indifference what's left of my privates, no longer having the desire to shake the fur right off that mangy bastard of a feline Tinkles, and bite the smile right off his smug face, as he taunts me so close I can smell his litter-box breath yet from the safety of that tree branch that I have repeatedly requested a saw from Larry . . .

Uh, right. What was I talking about?

As I look around the world I realize that others have it far more ruff. "Ruff!" Get it? Year-end regrets? Sure. Who doesn't have a few? I'm sorry I ate chunks out of the furniture. It seemed like a good idea at the time—it's hard to get roughage from slinky designer shoes. And I'm sorry for drinking out of the toilet, then frenching my housemates. Dozens and dozens of times. *-)

Rest assured, I'm aware that this is an addiction for which I am seeking help. These days, I'm taking things one toilet bowl at a time. Through the support group I belong to, I now realize that Larry, with his left-up lids, is an enabler. So, I will say my serenity prayer for this codependent human, as well.

This New Year, I resolve to increase my surveillance of the squirrels. More on this situation as it develops.

Food that falls from the sky remains the single greatest invention since sliced bologna. I hope you will all join me in praising the makers of gravity, a phenomenon that continues to perform spectacularly during every human meal.

Finally, let me state this: I know nothing of the hamster's disappearance. Likewise, the hunk of roast beef and the pound of butter. Further, I understand that a stranger in a red suit intends to show up unannounced on the premises one of these nights. With or without *cojones*—not on my watch, pal.

Let me close with some wishes for the next seven dog years:

> May your baths be short,
> Your walks be long,
> Every bush and hydrant,
> Filled with the aromas of the season.

DOG BLESS YOU,

🐾 🐾

Mr. Pooders

Amish Holiday Writings to Be Delivered by the Hand

Hello, You English,

 GLAD TIDINGS. The grain is bountiful and the harvest is blessed. And we have returneth to Yoder upon shunning the Thee Might Be Amish If . . . comedy tour: Did thee hear the one about the Amish stock broker? His stock portfolio was cows and sheep and his BlackBerry was an actual blackberry. We do not know what mean these jests but surely we do not care much for it. The Mennonites who laughed heartily and made sport were perhaps drunken on buttermilk wine.

Now am I finding time for life's simple pleasures like discipline, milking by the hand fifty cows each morning, and completion of *Amish Thunder*, my futuristic sci-fi tale of life in 1787 Pennsylvania. For thou who dost not know, *Amish Thunder* be the story of a plain man so named Ezekiel. Spurred on by the love of a good, plain woman, age thirteen, and their three children, brother Ezekiel's discovery of the God-sent invention of a hollowed pumpkin that, with the help of a magic buggy capable of being pulled by all matter of beasts including horse, goat, or perhaps ox, made possible the transport of water for several miles—water previously kept in one's plain hat and plain pockets before the discovery. *Amish Thunder* is a righteous tale surely to churn the butter of those who canst read. I will have copies for purchase at the spring quilting bee as soon as I canst locate the proper goose quills for transcription.

Wife giveth her tidings the same. May you find chores and Bible passages enough to sustain in your time of need.

We humbly pray for delivery of thine vain soul before eternal fire taketh thee.

IN PRAYER,

Jedadiah

FROM THE DESK OF DR. PHIL MCGRAW

Merry Christmas! How Ya'all Doing?

 LACK OF CHRISTMAS SPIRIT HAS OVERTAKEN cancer as the number-one cause of avoidable, preventable depression in American society. It's an epidemic-level problem. I'm Dr. Phil McGraw, and today we're going to give you what I like to call The Ultimate Holiday Solution: The Three Keys to Christmas Freedom. Now I know some of you have had lousy holidays in the past, but, as we say in Texas, you don't need red-and-white fur pants to do the two-step with an armadillo. What I'm trying to tell you is: Past performance does not equal now time and your mileage may vary. (Hold for applause.) Now, I am serious: When it comes to having Christmas freedom, failure is no accident, and, as we say in the McGraw household, "Failure is not a lifestyle choice."

When you get up tomorrow morning, take a minute to strip down to your birthday suit. Get out of those husky pants and look at yourself in the mirror. And I want you to see yourself not as someone who is overweight and depressed and should lay off the spiked eggnog and gingerbread men—I want you to lay off 'em all right, especially that eggnog—but right now you're going to see the festive someone just about boiling over with Christmas spirit. That's a person you want to become.

The first rule is that it's better to be festive alone than miserable with others. You want to stay with *ablers* and away from enablers. "Lord, how am I supposed to do that between now and Christmas Eve?" some of you are saying. "These are the only friends and family I got." That may be true, but here's the thing: "Sometimes you find pants that fit, sometimes you make the pants you have fit right." See what I'm saying?

You don't need the Big Bang Theory to follow rule number two. "Christmas spirit is a marathon, it's not a sprint." The season lasts five weeks, for crying out loud, so you're going to have to pace yourself. Simple as that.

And if you are feeling all depressed because there isn't a Wal-Mart stock room full of presents under your tree, rule number three says, "If you want more presents, you have to require more presence from yourself." What I'm trying to tell you is, "Sometimes you just got to give yourself what presents you wish someone else would give you." Maybe you're thinking, "Hey, that isn't right ol' Dr. Phil telling me to buy my own Christmas presents." What I am telling you is, "Do you want to be right, or do you want to be happy? Do ya want a tree full of presents, or don't ya?" I think we all know the answer to that. [Hold for whopping and more applause.]

Now, I wasn't born yesterday and tumbled out of a manger, but it seems to me that if you follow what I'm trying to tell you, then you're just going to have yourself one heck of a nice Christmas. [Hold for standing ovation.]

You all take care and I will see you in the new year.

Dr. Phil

Santa, You is the Shizzle

by Troy Sanders, Age Nine

Dear Santa,

I THOUGHT YOU MIGHT LIKE TO SEE A PAGE FROM MY blog. I'm sending you my letter in November, because I know you're big on promptness. I am, too. If anybody ever sends me a Christmas card that arrives after December 25th, I write back "Return to sender. Thanks, but you're a day late and a dollar short!" But, if it's a gift or money, I keep it. Hey, I'm not stupid.

Although last year was skimpy on presents (What was up with all the Pokemon stuff? Remember, I'm nine now.), I am so full of holiday spirit you can slice it up in chunks, put it in a blender, and make a mouth-watering smoothie. I wish it could be Christmas all year 'round. That way, I wouldn't ever have to take out the trash because garbagemen don't work on holidays.

Say, what do you call kids who are afraid of you?

"Claustrophobic." Ha! Ha! Get it? "Claustrophobic?"

How cold is it at the North Pole? Is it as cold as it is here? I looked out the window the other day and right away felt bad about making that bird feeder out of sheet metal instead of wood.

I bet there are worse things to be than a bird stuck to a feeder. For example, if you were a pirate with forty or fifty other toothless, drunk guys, I bet the holidays would be pretty darn depressing, especially if delousing were part of the deal. Probably everyone on board just regifts the same rusty hook hand every year, too. And don't even get me started about scurvy.

As you know, we have a pretty unconventional family, since it's mom who dresses up as Santa, and not just during Christmas. Hopefully you won't hold it against me personally. If you're even thinking about it, I want you to know, Santa, that I did my best to be good. Mom should be a detective, the way she's always on my case. I do admit there were a few off days. It was wrong of me to shoplift grandma's birthday present, but I think that getting caught with a Salad Shooter in one's pants is punishment enough. And bringing a real laser to a laser tag park seemed like a cool idea at the time. What the #&$*! was I thinking, right? You and I both can wonder a long time about that one. Same goes for downloading that mpeg named Elves Behaving Badly, that was nothing like the guys and I imagined and actually made us hurl.

The main thing is that most of the year I was good, and, in my heart, I know you won't forget about me. As Dad says, "Troy, you are a unique person just like everybody else."

So, please check out my attached Xmas Presents for Troy file, and thanks in advance for coming through with the goods.

Merry Christmas and Happy Hanukkah!

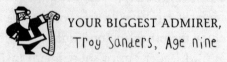

YOUR BIGGEST ADMIRER,
Troy Sanders, Age nine

P.S. You should think about getting Mrs. Claus some of those sweats that say NAUGHTY OR NICE across the backside. That would be cool.

Holiday Wishes to Troy Sanders, Age Nine,
FROM A NIGERIAN SCAM ARTIST

DEAR SIR,

THANK FOR YOUR CORRESPONDENCE on behalf of my esteemed husband St. Nicholas. However, be informed Sir that not only am I Mrs. Claus, but I am also widow to the former military head of state, late general Sani Abacha, who died suddenly as a result of cardiac arrest.

I must confess I do not know of this iPod of which you speak. However, one early morning, I was called by my late husband General Sani Abacha who at that time was the Commander-in-Chief of the Armed Forces and the Head of State of the Federal Republic of Nigeria. He took me around the apartment and showed me three metal boxes of money all in foreign currency.

My husband told me he was to use the money for the settlement of his personal royal guards on his self-succession bid and campaigns.

Upon his tragic and unexpected death, the new civilian government has insisted on probing my family's financial resources and has gazetted all our properties. Also, they recently seized all the family known funds abroad with the assistance of the British Government.

It is only this money US $60,000,000.00 (sixty million US dollars only) he deposited with the security company vault at Togo (Lome) that they cannot trace because the funds were deposited as an (antiquity) African artwork from Nigeria art gallery, the family intends to use this money for investment purpose to enable the family to start life all over again.

Therefore, the family is urgently in need of a very reliable investor participant that we could entrust with the certificate of deposit and PIN (personal identification number) to help us remove the funds since no names were used in securing the vault.

I got your name and contact address from our chamber of commerce and industry office in Lagos, Nigeria. If the proposal is acceptable to you, after getting the money out of the security company vault to your country, my family have agreed to offer you 25 percent of the total sum for the assistance you rendered to us and bank the family's own part of the funds and assist us in investing (with my approval) in a project as a front from there we can discuss the way forward, most especially now that my eldest son, Mohammed, and I are under pressure from the government.

Please kindly reach me by this e-mail, for more details on the logistics and modalities if you are interested in a partnership, so that we can arrange a meeting in (Lome) Togo at the security company.

Troy, age 9, I do not need to remind you of the absolute secrecy and confidentiality that this transaction demands. My son, Abba, will only be the one to tell you whenever it is possible to talk to me. If you are not interested, please kindly reply to me immediately to enable me to search for another interested partner.

**THANKS AND ACCEPT MY REGARDS.
MERRY CHRISTMAS TO YOU, TOO!**

Mariam Abacha (Alhaja)
Mrs. Claus, for the family

Note: You can as well call my son Abba (Claus) on his number 00 228 02 51 38 for more directives.

Holiday Musings from Inside the Desk

 ## of David Blaine

TO HONOR THIS SEASON, for the next ten days I will be shackled to a razor-tipped menorah chained to a lead Christmas tree inside a giant gyroscope and dropped out the bottom where I am suspended Christ-like fifty feet above my parents' house. Either I will break out, or be impaled by the menorah or crushed by the tree when I crash to the roof. Broadcast on ABC live on the night of December 12 from nine to ten o'clock. I worked really hard on this one. Enjoy. It will be beautiful.

If you believe that magic isn't real, well, you are wrong. Here's what I plan to do in the new year:
—Rip my buttocks off while guest hosting *The View*
—Remain submerged in 50,000 gallons of Chipolte sauce for one week

Still not a believer? Consider this: Those who complain about missing a meal or being bored. You have never really suffered or witnessed a loved one face death, smiling in your arms. I hope you are all so lucky one day. Think about it while I'm in the Chipolte sauce.

I do not consider myself as part of an individual species, planet, or galaxy. Just simply a human being and this is my exploration and now discovery of how strong we all are in mind, body, and spirit. To test this theory, I intend to:
—Spin for 3 days nonstop in an Olive Garden Never Ending Pasta Bowl (12 RPMs)
—Speed date myself nonstop for 6 hours

I know you'll join me. It's going to be a magical year.

Until then I leave you with this thought: The most courageous act a man inside a bubble can do is break wind. Think about it.

PEACE,

DB (to the power of one)

GOSH. Today was so beautiful the way the snow and wind whipped through the trees. All those beautiful gradations of white and gray. You just feel like you can do anything. I tried to get your father to build a snow fort like we used to do when you kids were little and living at home, but all he said was, "For crying out loud, Lydia. It's three in the morning. As if that had anything to do with the price of tea in China! Apparently, it's all *my* fault these holidays are such crap. Lunar eclipse happens more times than your father will admit he's wrong. He thinks he's clever and says things like "You should get new glasses for your stigmatatism." Clever, he ain't.

I wanted to shout out from the rooftops the glorious news of a new addition to our perfect, perfect family. If you'd listened to us about Leonard twelve years ago, you wouldn't be in this situation now. How on earth are you ever going to manage with four kids? Sounds like the other three haven't put a damper on bedroom activities. *<I;-) Maybe you kids can give tips to your father when you come home. Hee-hee! You are coming home, right? Where was I? Oh, thank God the Piggly Wiggly is open twenty-four hours. I know how you like

blueberry Pop-Tarts and now we have plenty. You'd think you'd get a discount for buying them by the case, but you'd be wrong. Oh, well! I showed everyone the sonogram you sent, and the cashier and several other shoppers agree that child is model material. It's never too early to plan for the future. Did I tell you that your brother is going to be the next Clarence Darrow? He intends to apply to law school next year and is serious this time. He even set up an office in the old playroom and it looks *official.* If I get rear-ended and end up in the hospital I know who I'm going to call! *-) Like I always say, "What the world needs is more ambulance chasers." Your brother's philosophy seems to be, "If, at first you don't succeed, you can always move back home . . . again." I'd rather be locked in a box with mimes than skulk around the house the way he does.

Well, I could go on and on but I think I'll surprise everyone with Pop-Tarts and a breakfast dish from every continent. Do you know if Antarctica is considered a continent and, if so, what they might serve there?

SINCERELY,

Your Dear Old Mom

(In case you forgot, I'm just the person who endured
86 hours of active labor in order to give you life.
Thanks for coming out sideways!)

XOXOOXOOXOXOXOXOXOXOXOX!

P.S. Hope the twins appreciated the socks for their birthdays. We didn't hear back. They cost a fortune to mail. What do you all want for Christmas? We're broke and cutting back this year.

P.P.S. Your father is driving me into an early grave.

THE Leidner Family Annual Christmas Poem

'T is the time of year again
To hear from even our most fair-weather friends.

May the season bring you warmth, joy, and good cheer
If the court orders Kirk back to AA, can he still drink beer?

Glad tidings we wish you from the bottom of our heart
Our Timmy is on the mend after he was impaled by a Jart.

Mama Beal keeps busy walking two miles each way
Past Shady Willow where she'll reside one day.

Since he stopped bowling things haven't been the same with Lou
Ask your doctor if Cialis is right for you.

Across the street they bought a new front door
Lots of red stained glass
Just goes to show
Money can't buy class.

Our friends, the Carters, have moved away,
In their place, a family of five.
The neighborhood's changed—what can we say?
Their name is Twang. They speak Thai.

Sandy still hangs out with her pal Chris
A husky girl who manages nights at the Golden Arch.
In May they moved into a condo
Now, they're never apart.

Last Christmas the grandkids surprised Lou unloading a sack
Now, they think Santa has plumber's crack.

Well, time to wrap this up and clean up this place
Don't forget to spread holiday joy
By keeping a smile plastered on your face
Especially if you see Aunt Alice, and her new boy toy.

Love, Bev

Holiday Greetings 2007!

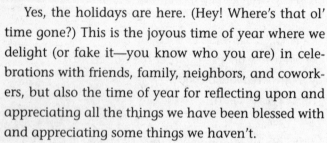

Dearest Family, Friends, and Others

HERE IS MY LETTER TO THE WORLD!

'Tis the season! Am I right? To be jolly! Who's with me? Fa la la la la, la la la, la!

Yes, the holidays are here. (Hey! Where's that ol' time gone?) This is the joyous time of year where we delight (or fake it—you know who you are) in celebrations with friends, family, neighbors, and coworkers, but also the time of year for reflecting upon and appreciating all the things we have been blessed with and appreciating some things we haven't.

ALL IN ALL, OUR LIFE IS GREAT. I fill my day knitting socks for the aged. Devon recently received the promotion of a lifetime and is now Junior Vice President of VP Operations. Tyler was All-Conference quarterback this year and Tiffany, who just turned twelve, was delighted to receive her early acceptance to Harvard. It's amazing how they find time to study, between all the volunteer activities, holding part-time jobs to save for their educations, and being captain of the football team and cheerleading squad.

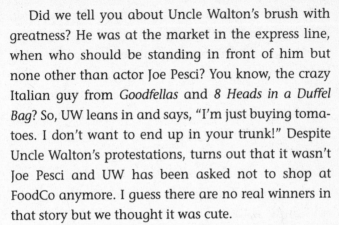

Did we tell you about Uncle Walton's brush with greatness? He was at the market in the express line, when who should be standing in front of him but none other than actor Joe Pesci? You know, the crazy Italian guy from *Goodfellas* and *8 Heads in a Duffel Bag*? So, UW leans in and says, "I'm just buying tomatoes. I don't want to end up in your trunk!" Despite Uncle Walton's protestations, turns out that it wasn't Joe Pesci and UW has been asked not to shop at FoodCo anymore. I guess there are no real winners in that story but we thought it was cute.

I don't want to get on a soapbox but, this year, in particular, I have been aware of how arbitrary it is as to where we are born and in what circumstances we live our lives. For those of us born in a bountiful country and, if we are lucky, into a prosperous family, life gets off to a promising start. But for those born into far too many families, in places like Darfur, Port-au-Prince, Sudan, Fallujah, or many parts of the Deep South, life is not so easy regardless of whether one has, say, a spastic colon, which would be the least of a person's troubles.

Everyday, these people must somehow manage to lick the dust and filth off themselves and crawl out of the cosmic corn-cob crib to face the uncertain day. For so many people on this planet, *accident of birth* means the difference between a life of comfort and privilege and a struggle with no opportunity to acquire a state-of-the-art boat, a beaut that comes complete with twin 2500 hp inboard motors, and really leaves an impressive wake up at the lake!

Of course, being blessed is all relative, and it is human nature to complain about things like rush-hour traffic or free pizza samples gone cold at Costco. But, at this time of year, when we turn our attention outward to others, the accident of our birth and the opportunities it affords us should give us food for thought and deep appreciation. I, for one, am profoundly grateful for certain members of my wonderful family, without whom no amount of the success and fame that currently envelops me would mean anything. I am grateful for my health, and for the fact that I wake up each morning in this wonderful country. The U S of A. I am grateful for the fact that I have a roof over my head and food in my flat stomach and that my gifted and charming children stand a pretty good chance of prospering better than most of the neighbors' kids. Truly, we are the lucky ones. And one of the burdens of being one of the lucky ones is to show kindness to others less lucky, which is a nice segue to what I want to talk about next.

The Kindness Olympics were a high point for all of us this year. I was so moved by your selflessness and compassion that I wanted to respond in kind this holiday season with something that would have meaning to all of you, as well. You know the saying, "Give a man a fish and he will eat for a day. Teach a man to fish and he will eat for a lifetime"? Well, one of the organizations we all volunteer for is the Learn to Fish Foundation. They provide to people in need videos from *The Bass Master* television series Devon is so fond of, outdated video-fishing-game software, and back issues of *Field and Stream*.

Almost every child is precious. So, you would be as shocked as I was to learn that there are kids in some inner cities who have never felt the joy of a tug on their line, never held a rod? I know that many of you have already sent some wonderful gifts for which we thank you. However, in lieu of reciprocating, this year, we will forgo the rampant commercialism of the season by making a donation from our *Outdoor Life* magazine collection to Learn to Fish, in honor of you. This holiday season some underprivileged families living in our community, will receive praise, good wishes, and some handy reading material in celebration of you.

So, from my gifted family to you and yours, a special seasonal greeting for peace, kindness, and our very best wishes for a bountiful, fulfilling, and exciting year ahead!

BEST,

Julie McConnell

Filling and Loathing on Elm Street

Dear Neighbors,

SORRY FOR THIS INTRUSION INTO YOUR MAILBOX. In previous years, we would have shared all the goings on in the Henderson house. However, as many of you know, the events of the recent Thanksgiving have so disgusted and concerned us that we feel compelled to send this painful update out instead. Please believe us when we say that we would never have put that pie on the windowsill to cool if we thought anything like this could happen.

The tragedy certainly would never have occurred if those Hollywood producers had taken into account how impressionable the kids who watch their movies are. We are happy to report from Collin's Mom that he is home from the hospital and is recovering quickly from his minor burns. At the very least, the despicable people who made that terrible movie *American Pie* owe us and the Griffins an apology, and should cover Collin's medical bills. Anyone who thinks it's funny to teach teenagers how to pleasure themselves with hot pastry—well, they aren't funny. They are sick individuals in my book.

Thanks to all of you who chipped in with the yard sale and the bake sale (no, we didn't sell apple pie). We raised $546 to help with Collin's recovery. There is some good news to report. Collin plans to be back in school as soon as the publicity dies down and the bandages come off. Nancy asked me to pass along to little Tessy, "Thanks so much for the offer, but this isn't really the kind of cast you can sign."

SINCERELY,

The Balthmore Family

To: Students, Colleagues, Family
Fr: Professor Lawrence Tobin
Re: In lieu of a holiday epistle

The Economics of Christmas

*Y*OU HAVE TWO TMX ELMOS; you want Bling Bling Barbie; you set out to find another shopper who has Bling Bling Barbie and wants a TMX Elmo

- **Anarchism:** You have two TMX Elmos. You steal your neighbor's cat.

- **Socialism:** You have two TMX Elmos. The government takes one and gives it to someone else.

- **Communism:** You have two TMX Elmos. The government takes both of them and gives you back the box.

- **Totalitarianism:** You have two TMX Elmos. The government takes them and denies they ever existed. TMX Elmos are banned.

- **Capitalism:** You have two TMX Elmos. You sell them both on eBay and buy a Hummer.

- **Fascism:** You have two TMX Elmos. The government shoots one, and sells you back the other one.

I will see you all in January.
REGS,
Tobin, PhD

A SPECIAL MESSAGE OF THE SEASON
from Dr. Vladimir Bonacio

My Friends,

CAN YOU BUY HAPPINESS? Maybe. Or maybe you can make that inner misery just a little more beautiful.

Season's greetings from Dr. Vladimir Bonacio, your neighborhood board-licensed cosmetic surgeon. I'm here to put a new smile on your new face. A truly wise man once said that it's what's inside that counts. That's why new silicon liquid-gel breast implants are the perfect gift for your loved one. Beauty is only skin deep, so, show your wife, mom, or even dear old sis just how much you truly care. It's a gift that keeps on giving, and is sure to have others looking at her new chest or buttocks and saying, "Look what she got for Christmas!"

In this season of selfless giving, don't you owe it to yourself to ring in the new year with a new face? Our mission is to empower men and women with surgical augmentation. Stop in to see the latest trends for the new year. We have many before-and-after photos you're sure to enjoy.

Free laser hair removal with a purchase of a facelift.

Ask about our Botox and silicone two-for-one special.

Have it done in the morning. Be dancing by dinner!

HAPPY HOLIDAYS

DERMASURG
(Formerly the Colon Hydrotherapy Institute)
TRULY A CUT ABOVE.

Take a Christmas Bow
HOLIDAY HIT REVIEW FROM NEW JERSEY!

WELL, WELL. It's been an eventful year any way you slice it: Britney Spears is so played out I don't know what I ever saw in her. Luckily, I found a way to fill the void by becoming a cabaret musical-comedy star!!! Yes, the acting bug has truly bitten me and it turned out to be a short hop from *Brigadoon* and "You're in Town!" at the Schenectady Community Center to *Star Wars: The Musical* just 282 blocks from The Great White Way!! I miss most of you like crazy and would love to have you come see the show, but we are on a limited five-day engagement.

Dale asked about coming to visit, but I am currently renting with two other promising actors, a closet of a studio apartment in Elizabethport, New Jersey. Unfortunately, it is not a walk-in and my closetmates have become a couple after a night of intense soul-searching.

You would think you'd get more of New Jersey for $700 a month but you would be wrong, and if you think a bunk bed won't fit in a closet, well, you're mostly right. Luckily, we manage pretty well with the buddy system and by sleeping in shifts. Off-off-off Broadway is a great opportunity and an actor's dream, but sometimes I still miss life as a singing cauliflower at Spumoni.

Thank you so much for all of your generous gifts, cards, and cash. Given my dedication to my art and financial situation, I have decided not to participate in the commercialism of the holidays. After all, Jesus Christ Superstar *is* the reason for the season. I often wonder what extraterrestrials think of all the garish displays. And so my special gift to you are the timeless words of Moby:

> No one can stop us now
> 'Cause we are all made of stars.

Happy Holidays and the very best wishes for a peaceful, joyful, and dramatic New Year.

MORE ANON.

Your Stephen

CELEBRITY MEA CULPA
✶ CHRISTMAS LETTER ✶

F OR ANYONE I HAVE EVER WRONGED IN THE PAST, present, or future, what can I say but, "my bad." Jewsus said this is the season for forgiveness and to let bygones be bygones. This seems like as good a time as any to apologize for things I said or am about to say here or later at Mel Gibson's house warming party/rally that might be taken out of context and get blown up way out of proportion. I have battled the disease of alcoholism for all of my adult life, and profoundly regret my horrific relapses now and in the future. I'm certain that my legions of beak-nosed, watermelon-eating, taco-toting fans will surely understand no matter what their sexual orientation. Clearly, stupid (Jewish-Black-Latino) (bastards/bitches) intend to get their panties in a twist over nothing. Meanwhile, they would be better served if they spent less time controlling world currencies-lacking personal initiative-sneaking across the border) to take jobs we true Americans would eagerly accept as soon as we are paid twenty-six dollars an hour for plucking chickens in a factory or picking oranges. These people disproportionately represent Knicks season ticket holders-song-and-dance finalists-hotel-cleaning-service staffing. But, hey, any woman who feels that I have offended her is welcome back to my hotel room to discuss the transgression over drinks. That's just how I am.

Rest assured, my words have been or will be misconstrued. That does not excuse either my insensitivity or a blood-alcohol content of .28. I am deeply ashamed of everything I said. I deeply regret it. Also, I take this opportunity to apologize to the staff of Red Lobster who were the brunt of my belligerent behavior. TJ McSneezy's is a fine establishment and, indeed, Jill the bodacious but apparently frigid server's quick action to drop a sizzling jumbo shrimp platter into my open fly probably saved me from myself.

Merry Christmas or whatever it is you people celebrate. Or as Dad likes to call Hanukkah, Jewish Christmas. I guess that would make Kwanzaa black Hanukkah. Or whatever.

Holiday Regards,

inebriated celebrity x

Satan's Greetings from Lucifer and Family

PLEASE NOTE THAT THIS IS OUR VERY FIRST SHOT at writing a holiday letter but, don't worry, you won't need an insulin injection to read it.

Wake me when Christmas is over. Traditionally, this has been the cruelest month for the Lucifer family. It's always "Prince of Evil this," and "Prince of Evil that," but does anyone have us on their secret Santa list? I know the holidays are supposed to be about more than materialism; still, it would be nice to finally find the flame-retardant furniture that we always wish for under the tree.

Our mail is always mixed up with Santa's—you'd think we'd get along better by now. After all, are we really so different? Are we not two guys of the world who do celebrity endorsements? (He has Coca-Cola, I have Duke University and Underwood Deviled Ham.) Not only that, we share an anagram, wear red suits, and are surrounded by tiny minions. And we both answer wish lists—although, admittedly, the costs may vary.

Someone commented that I am beginning to look like Mickey Rourke. Let me just say that the pressure to keep the home fires burning and *kids* will do that to you. On that topic, many thanks to those of you who wrote to express shock in seeing our daughter Rainbow in a *Girls Behaving Badly* video. Rest assured she is in counseling and now understands that, if you expose yourself on national television, it should be for monetary compensation. So, we cross our fingers and hope for the best. Silly me for thinking this was the worst possible thing that could happen this year, but discovering that our eldest, Shannon, joined a Christian rock band certainly took that cake. Following an incident in which she spoke in tongues and attempted to poke me in the eye with a crucifix, Shannon got my famous "mess with devil, and you get the horns" speech and will be home-schooled next year.

Thank Baal, Trevor has turned out so well. I had to pull a few strings, but last week he was accepted early decision at Dartmouth.

So, it's not all complaints. We still enjoy our summers in Las Vegas, where the relatively cooler weather is a nice change of pace. Driving a Hummer takes some getting used to, but I have to say that any place that's still hot enough for kids to make sand into glass on the sidewalk is all right by me.

The only downer of this past year was having the TiVo out of order in the condo, so Celine and I were stuck watching endless loops of *Diagnosis*

Murder. I swore I would give Dick Cheney his soul back if he would just send over a repairman, but apparently Dick's way too swamped running the country. The Bastard. Just for fun, I should prank call him at the hospital with "Do you smell gas?" or pose as an insurance rep about to raise his health insurance deductible. But that gets old.

Despite constant solicitations from developers, I think we're going to stay put down here for another year. Hell has its drawbacks, for sure, and the neighborhood has changed, but frankly, I would miss the lava. Seriously, who wouldn't?

Celine and I have dreamed of the day when we would join the ranks of downsizing empty-nesters but, the other day in yoga class, it hit me that, "When you dance with the devil and you are the devil, you dance alone."

Well, there's always fire at the end of the tunnel, so I hope to catch up with all of you in the New Year (if you know what I mean).

HAPPY HOLIDAYS!

The Lucifers

GRAMPY FALLS IN HOLIDAY VIOLENCE!

The police officer said it was a childish prank that almost turned deadly. Someone who is too gutless to come forward put a vibrator in this year's Thanksgiving turkey.

As soon as Hal cut into it the bird started bouncing around and, what with the house full of people, you can imagine the panic.

I heard someone screaming (later, they said it was me) and my first thought was, "Oh my God! This turkey is possessed! I should have shopped at the Safeway, like I always do." Satan's fowl seemed to rise up on its hind legs, and that's when Grandpa leaped into action. I need not remind anyone that it was Grandpa who saw action as a clerk in the South Pacific during WWII. The metal plate in gramp's head is a constant reminder of that stapler accident. Always one to make the best of a bad situation, he uses a refrigerator magnet to keep his to-do list extra-handy. Anyhow, grandpa longs for those exciting days and watching him wrestle Satan's fowl into submission, taking out a serving table on the way to the floor, I remember thinking, "At least he'll die doing what he loved best." Luckily, the paramedics were able to revive him, but they kept him overnight at St. Mary's under observation just as a precaution.

All's well that ends well, I suppose, and I have promised not to point fingers. Phyllis has it on good authority that Lorraine and Neal are some kind of swingers. I, for one, am not surprised. The police officer didn't have enough information to make the arrest, but prison is what they deserve. Straighten them out quick. May they rot in hell for ruining my turkey.

GOOD NEWS!
LARRY TURNS FIFTY!

Larry celebrated turning the landmark age of fifty by buying the 1967 Firebird he always wanted. The car isn't actually running (no engine), but Larry insists it was the deal of the century and couldn't be passed up.

Larry is taking an automotive shop course at the local community college, and believes this will be the perfect father-and-son project for him and the neighbor's kid Duane. Despite the new

toupee, and rumors to the contrary, Larry is *not* in the middle of a full-blown midlife crisis.

SON ROGER'S LOW SPERM COUNT DOOMS HOPE FOR GRANDKIDS

We don't know how many more good years we have left but, it's his life, as he's told us a thousand times. If he wants to reduce his chances by wearing bikini briefs, it isn't our say. Then again, what can you say about someone who joined the Navy in order to learn how to swim? Or somebody whose idea of funny is going into a Kmart dressing room, then yelling, "Hey! We're all out of toilet paper in here!"

ROBBY'S CORNER, AS REPORTED TO MOM

Besides computers, I enjoy ham radio and belong to two ham-radio clubs. Saturday mornings I go on a ham-radio fox hunt. Someone hides anywhere west of Clearwater and transmits from his ham radio. The contest is who will find this fox first, using radio signals. I, Robby, explore a lot of conservation land and parks and trails in search of good places for the fox to hide. The end.

STEVE'S BLOG TELLS IT LIKE IT IS

Kudos to Steve for his scathing exposé of the Special Olympics in the *Clearwater Free Press Circular*. You can't tell me some of those kids haven't crossed the line. I don't care how many of them picket our house.

TRAGEDY STRIKES THE COOPERS

Our neighbors Phil and Lenore have always been traditionalists. Store-bought is not good enough for them. (Steve calls their annual neighborhood barbecue, "The blowhard's trip to Bountiful." Hee-hee!) They say it's not about being better than other people.

We will see if they still say the same thing when they get back from St. Joseph's Hospital. Word to the wise, if you buy a Christmas tree from one of those cut-it-yourself places, make sure you check it out carefully before you set it up, and invite a lot of people over for a tree-trimming party. Apparently, killer bees take a while to wake up but when they do, they sure don't like flashing lights.

Here's wishing our dear neighbors, Phil and Lenore, and everyone else invited to that tree-trimming party a speedy recovery. God bless.

CHRISTMAS PRAYER

Here's hoping Jesus will lead all mankind out of the darkness in the new year! And keep those letters to McDonald's coming. We think our idea of McManger toys in every Happy Meal is a good one! Collect them all!

AMEN!

 THIS HOLIDAY SEASON IS BITTERSWEET, but I'm bound and determined to see the silver lining.

My failure to turn Just Ointments! into a mall franchise shocked all of us. It was a sad day when the store burned down on Halloween, just days before the fire insurance was to expire. The police said that pranksters don't usually rig flaming bags of dog p**p to explode. In hindsight, we sure made a lot of mistakes, and owning an ointment shop might have been chief among them. People with skin lesions can be some of the crankiest, most unpleasant clients on God's green earth, even if they are dedicated repeat customers. But, on the bright side, I must tell you that we learned so much about owning a retail business. While there are no do-overs, I plan to put all of these lessons to good use when we open our new store for kids, Just Ringworm.

SOME SADNESS & SOME GLADNESS

Sadly, we've had our share of health troubles this year. This latest surgery to restore Phil's saliva gland was unsuccessful. He has been valiant throughout this trauma, and some good has come from his long struggle. I'm happy to report that Phil has redoubled his efforts to patent synthetic salsa flavored Drool®.

For those of you who remember, let me just say, "Do not underestimate that man's determination." As I've said a thousand times, "If man were meant to walk on the sun, my husband is meant to go first."

Many of you will remember Phil's efforts a few years back to find a cure for our hamster, Raisin, who suffered from ADD. Unfortunately, Raisin disappeared one morning before work could be completed, so Phil was forced to abandon his quest. Now, it is Phil's dream to ease the pain of thousands who are unable to produce their own saliva and must suffer in silence. In any case, I long for the day when Phil will be able to clear his throat without my assistance.

I'm happy to report that a cyst was removed from my ovary without a hitch. The surgeon even carved his initials on my uterine wall! I'm not much for graffiti or tattoos, but I can't help but feel honored. As you can see from the photo below, I even treated myself to a tummy tuck that is healing nicely and has taken years off my waistline.

Here is some information courtesy of Dr. Rebma Sdnabsuh of the Fallopian Health Information Center, which I know you will appreciate:

CYSTS are no joke and a tummy tuck can spice things up in the boudoir. Be sure to get regular pelvic exams. Some cysts can be the size of tennis balls.

Anyway, I'm not saying we wish we never had kids but there are times . . . I'm mostly just kidding, of course. Tee-hee. The therapist says if Timmy wants to pretend that two pounds of pork loin is a Tickle Me Elmo doll, fine. *Fine?* Who am I to stifle his creativity? Let him walk around wearing my un-mentionables on top of his pants. I'm sick of it. How they ever talked me into adopting that spider monkey is beyond me. It's a mean drunk and flings monkey feces around the living room like nobody's business. Here's hoping Timmy makes good on his threat to go live on the bottom of the ocean with his monkey.

We are still angry at Dr. Steve, the optometrist who told Timmy that the twinkle in Santa's eyes was due to cataracts.

Many of you commented about seeing the front-page newspaper photo of the Secret Service wrestling Grandpa to the ground. I would like to thank everyone for their many kind prayers and calls of concern after Grandpa's arrest following his wardrobe malfunction during a No Child Left Behind rally. We have told him a thousand times to get proper suspenders. And to wear underpants at all times. Not just on Sundays. (He claims Timmy stole them all to make slingshots.)

Personally, I don't think they need to make a federal case about it but, apparently, they disagree. Grandpa's hearing before a Federal judge is in three weeks.

Finally, what holiday letter would be complete without our annual recipe for Festive Hobo Dinners. Each meal is like a treasure hunt for the kids! As you know, this is a tradition passed down from a generation of Percivals who sought their fortune by clinging to the bottoms of westbound trains. While we no longer enjoy the meals ourselves, we still take time to make two dozen or so each Christmas that we secretly leave on the doorsteps of those we deem to be less fortunate.

MERRY CHRISTMAS!
The Percival Family

FESTIVE HOBO DINNERS

Six empty soda cans
*One pound scrapple (Jimmy Dean pork links
   will do in a pinch)*
One package tiny marshmallows
One can French-cut string beans
One can beets

Preheat oven to 350° (or pull over your RV to open hood).

Open the tops of all of the soda cans with a can opener (do not try jamming everything into the sipping hole like Kelly did a few years back).

Mix together all ingredients. Pour into the 6 soda cans evenly. Place in oven or on top of carburetor. Warning: Do not put cans in microwave! Heat twenty minutes, or until next rest stop.

SERVES 6 HOBOS OR 8 OF THE NEIGHBORS' KIDS

MERRY CHRISTMAS
from Crugersville

As usual, it has been a fun and exciting year in Crugersville.

I have often said that if you throw a chair on national television, the world will beat a path to your trailer. Judging by the reaction of folks around town, it's only a matter of time before the endorsements and life-story rights start rolling in, following our appearance on *Jerry Springer*. I think we all came off pretty damn good. As Dad always used to say, "When you have a dream you have to follow it no matter where it takes you." Cleveland, in his case.

I guess the biggest news is that Linwood turned ten this week. As you know, Linbob and me are fervent believers in unintelligible design—the concept that God the Creator has a plan for all things but most people are too gosh-darn ignorant to understand it. So, we have formed a home school for children who have been pulled from home schools that are too permissive. Case in point, children who march around to Barney who we all know exists mainly to test our faith. I guess there are a growing number of like-minded individuals in Colorado. Still, it was quite a shock for Linbob and me when we were named to the Crugersville School Advisory Board.

This board, and now us, is in charge of making the recommendations for all the textbooks in the classrooms. We review boxes and boxes of textbooks to make sure they are suitable for all schools in the valley. Not many pass mustard, I can tell you that! I'm still working at the Big K. My position is still very high profile, since it's my job to polish the blue light that shines that much brighter now that Martha Stewart is back in society. Can you say *total major stress*?

Momma managed to ride out this year's hurricane in Coco Del Resedo. She has a new street address, on account of the double wide getting blowed one street over. We'll keep you posted if she gets moved again. By the way, she did a-okay in the colitis settlement. Hallelujah!

Our Linsteven just turned fourteen. We think he may have OCD, like I read about, so we're trying to get him on meds. He spends hours at a time in the bathroom running through the Zest and Jergens like they're going out of style. When we ask him what he's doing, he says, "Washing up!"

This year was not all fun and games. We said good-bye to Mr. March, who was ten days shy of making it into the *Guinness Book of Records* as the world's oldest crossing guard. It is truly a blessing that he forgot his glasses that fateful day and never saw the semi that sent him to the pearly gates.

Shout-out to Debbie in Scranton. I don't think you should be on Mason's butt all the time about the racetrack. He's bound to get better at the bets. After all, it's only money. As for you complaining whenever he comes home broke, I would remind you of what Momma Clarke (a woman who could make broken glass out of lemonade) always said, "Only a quitter quits, you big fat quitter!"

We carry you in our prayers. Enjoy the blessed holiday full of the knowledge of the love that the God Almitey has for you!

LOVE AND BLESSINGS OF THE SEASON TO ALL OF YOU!

Linella

Holiday Skinheads at Starbucks

by KEATON MANDY,
Poet in Training

Starbucks whirs and hums
Bustling with business.
I don't want to lose my place
A cog in the mocha java machine.
So I leave my work
Spread out and go for
Coffee
O sweet Venti.
Maybe from the Kigabah Estate
Of Papua New Guinea.

I am
Next to order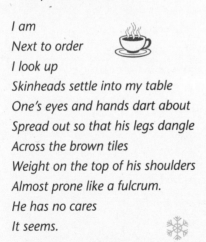
I look up
Skinheads settle into my table
One's eyes and hands dart about
Spread out so that his legs dangle
Across the brown tiles
Weight on the top of his shoulders
Almost prone like a fulcrum.
He has no cares
It seems.

The other is as languid
In his wife beater T-shirt
He moves inside tight, invisible boxes

Someone who has done time
Knows economy of space
Sitting chair turned backwards
Arms casual
Folded easy
On the chair back
One arm is a maze of ink with the word WHITE
Vertical through the center of entwined figures
Swastikas with wings,
Little cartoon birds in flight.

There's a laptop in that bag of mine
What the hell was I thinking?

"Hi. Would you like to try a gingerbread or pumpkin latte
only available for a limited time?"
No.

I chance completing my order
Chastising myself when I glance away
Distracted by the clatter of a hard plastic cup
Falling
And a pretty girl with dark eyes
Plush, fleshy body.
A small pillow of baby fat swaddling her navel
UCLA across her ass.

Two nerds with black-framed glasses
Practice pitches
"It's Indiana Jones Meets The Matrix."
"Uh huh," the other nerd says
Right.

I forcibly relax my shoulders and do my best amble back to
the table.
I practice
"Hey, guys."
And go with "How'zitgoin'?"
In my best Ricky Ticky voice.
Wish I knew jujitsu.
Elvis overhead croons "My Baby Left Me"
The Sun Sessions
Now, "Blue Moon."

No eye contact from the pair
Not even a smirk.
Just the half beat we all wait
Quick eyes and slow
Before sliding out from their chairs
Formerly my chairs
Stalking out like killers
Among sheep.
That really a caramel mocha he has?

I smile inside
When they're
In the parking lot.

So those are skinheads.
This gingerbread latte is delish.

MySpace
for the Holidays

I'M SORRY TO DISAPPOINT ALL OF YOU WHO ARE logging in for another exciting entry in my tell-all blog novel, *I Know Who You Did Last Summer*, based on my summer-camp-counselor journal. The novel will be back in the new year, and I promise to reveal:

☛ Why you never want to sit in the Camp Puma catamaran with anything less than a haz-mat suit after what Rachel and Scott did there one moonlit night.

☛ Why Angelina Jolie is the cause of global warming.

☛ The difference between burlap sacks and burlap sex and, trust me, you don't want to find out the way Lindsey X. did.

☛ The mystery of who gave Andrea panty crickets (it's not who you think).

But, today, I plan to imbue you with Christmas spirit and New Year's resolutions. I know what many of you are saying, "The more things change, the more I want to go on the South Beach diet." All you muffin tops know what I'm talking about. Trust me, change is good. For me, change is daring and carefree. Suddenly, I feel like being daring and carefree. Well . . . I'm not crazy, so as daring and carefree as I ever get. Here are the things I did today to start down the path to being daring and carefree.

- Decided to earn extra spending money by selling my holiday cheer on eBay. Withdrew after Mom used the Buy It Now option.

- Decided to be a mensch (am I spelling that right, Sarah?) and water my sister-in-law's flowers while she's away. Then I remembered how she said my hips were "too bumpy" for pleather. Somehow, I found myself adding salt to the water. That's certainly carefree in my book, but then I felt guilty when the plants wilted so I went out and bought her all new flowers.

- Wore my red-and-green flannel jammies with the Christmas trees on them all day. Just the top. Pajama bottoms you say? I wore them out to the mailbox and waved to Mrs. Nieder who nearly crashed into a parked car.

- Tried turning on the hose while a bit too near a rake. Inspector Clouseau and Sideshow Bob already rode that gag into the ground, you say? How else am I going to get the new Invisalign braces? How many of you caught the world premiere event on YouTube?

- ☞ Respect the privacy and feelings of others. Like when Brittany Delaney came to me all in tears because she said now that Candice was my NBF she felt like a third wheel (which she is). I could have gone off on Brittany, but I didn't. Instead, I put on my Miss Sensitivity hat. I explained that her friendship was just like last year's model mistake—perfectly fine for most people but a little less desirable for obvious reasons. Certainly no reflection on her.

- ☞ I resolve not to gossip—except about people I don't like.

- ☞ I resolve to be a better person—except in those situations when being a worse person works out better for me or gets me out of a jam.

Thus, ends my first day of my New Year's resolution of living on the edge, trying to be daring and carefree. I feel good about it, really. Learned a lot about myself and was cool with it, and on the edge. . . . Oh who am I kidding? I'm as on the edge as a spork. Time for some ice-cream therapy. What should I order? Hello, Cherry Garcia and butter crunch, my old friends. BTW—Did you hear about Jennifer? Can you say HPT results negative but very close call.

 HAPPY HOLIDAYS! GOD BLESS!

Debbie (aka Dangerous Destiny Girl 186)

HOW YOU ALL DOING. MY DEAR BROTHA?

NOW, YOU KNOW I'M ALL ABOUT TALKING AND I ain't much for no letter writing. So, I will keep it short and real. We know you are off in the Middle East fighting and whatnot, so we are gonna let you off the hook, cut you some slack for missing Momma's funeral. Can't you at least come home for Christmas? Don't they have no Christmas and whatnot over there? They're just lucky it isn't me in those Marines. I don't take no clowning like they've got going on in DC. Somebody should tell those high-and-mighty people to get off the cross, 'cause somebody else needs the wood. I swear to God.

Anyways, I would like to tell you that I honored every one of Momma's requests but the one. Apparently, that military has some rules and regulations about burying somebody face down. Are they for real? What do they care how Momma gets buried? As you know, Daddy was in the service, too, and he is buried in the plot twelve feet deep. Momma is at six feet on top of Daddy. So, Momma said, "Long as we gotta go through Eternity together in the same plot, we might as well face one another and get cozy like old times." I guess they will just have to settle for doing spoons, instead.

If you can't make it home for Christmas, be sure to know we love you and we miss you. So, don't you go getting foolish and stick your neck out. We're all proud of you no matter. Like Momma always said, "Live so the world won't owe you nothing." So come home safe to make some more babies for Auntie Toni to spoil.

LOVE,
Your sister, Toni

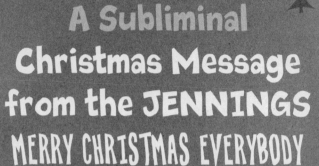

A Subliminal Christmas Message from the JENNINGS
MERRY CHRISTMAS EVERYBODY
(except Margaret)!

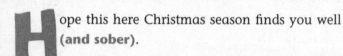

Hope this here Christmas season finds you well **(and sober)**.

We've been pretty busy around here, just like some of you **(losers)**.

Last winter flew by **(depression)**. In February, Wayne and I made it to the time share **(losing our mind)** in McClellanville. I so was relieved **(pissing myself)** in April when my health **(bladder infection)** improved. Oh, happy day **(painful discharge)**! Summer was hot as hell **(where Margaret is going)**. It was too hot for **(sex)** gardening, so I told **(our gardener Pedro)** Wayne we'll just have to **(have sex)** buy our **(hung like a)** zucchini from the store this year. He moped straight through to September but it was for the best **(sex I've ever had)**.

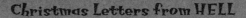

Fall was uneventful **(Pedro deported)**. Doctor's appointments, fantasy lottery league **(swingers' club)**. Wayne lost his job but we're okay and not looking for a handout **(donate)**. Oh, and we attended a dog marriage in Winder, GA. **(What a bitch!)** Real nice. We had a swell Thanksgiving **(new gardener)**.

This month, Wayne is making extra money as a department-store Santa **(drunken clown)**, but I tell him his beard looks distinguished **(smells like old cold cuts)**. No wonder all those cute kids **(little bastards)** pull it something fierce. The money is good **(petty theft)**. Last week, we were coming back from his shift **(armed robbery)**, when the motor stopped by Lake Sherman **(police shootout)**. We were five hours late getting home **(Bonnie and Clyde)**. It cost over three thousand dollars **(gas station stickup)** for a new motor. Why not! It's only money we don't have **(hostages)**!

In closing **(serving life sentence)**, we want to wish you a Merry Christmas **(send hack saw)** and a Happy New Year **(bolt cutters)**!

LOVE (conjugal visits),

Wayne and Jenny Jennings

Toddler
Yuletide Message

Now, it's almost Christmas. Everybody better think about the important stuff.

If you see reindeer poop in the snow, don't touch it.

Santa will you break my roof? I hope not.

If I was Santa, I would give kids so many presents.

I will make the chimney slippery for you, Santa. Don't fall off the roof.

If Rudolph was a dinosaur that would be funny.

I will leave the cookies, okay? Maybe you can try cheese sticks.

BYE-BYE.
Sophia, now three,
no, four, years old

My Walden Pond Holiday Blog by Henry David Thoreau

November 21, 1853

Three key rules for living well on a frozen pond: ❧ Never attend a cockfight naked. ❧ If you attend a cockfight naked, make sure there's plenty of good spirits on hand. ❧ What was I saying?

November 22, 1853

The scented candles Herman Melville has left behind has done little to lift my dark spirits. Already, the wind howls and the snow piles up outside this dwelling. Fashion me a flying machine from iron and wood and I will leave this forsaken lake, flying to Ye Olde Jamba Juice posthaste. O, sweet matcha green-tea shots!

November 23, 1853

Perhaps Herman is correct and the feng shui is not correct in this cabin. Must make inquiries with Brother Kaczynski how well he fares in that birdhouse he calls a home.

November 24, 1853

My stomach sated with glorious Mother turkey I would sing to the heavens the praises of this very special day, my eyes mist, and there is a lump in my throat.

Bits of congealed gravy, I believe.

Content am I, sealed tight in a warm blanket and fart cloud like a Dutch oven.

November 30, 1853

The mass of men lead lives of quiet desperation. Others break holiday bread with squirrels, birds, and woodchucks. So true.

December 3, 1853

Upon the publication of *Civil Disobedience* my life has gone supernova. I am serious. The Billabong contracts and the bling-bling. Truly, it is so awesome. Let's face it, my career is about to blow up. Everyone from the OC (Old Coventry) will be superjealous.

Note to self: Trademark the Transcendental Power Diet (tobacco and coffee). Idea may be gold—we are talking Gutenberg bible dollars. Also, Thoreau limited edition Docker jeans.

December 14, 1853

Whenever I see the lot of some worse than mine I must laugh. For isn't that truly what life is all about?

December 17, 1853

We can make liquor to sweeten our lips.

And sleeping draught hewn from pumpkins and parsnips and walnut-tree chips.

Cool.

I rejoice that my secret Santa is a beaver.

December 22, 1853

The son of a tanner, John Brown, claims to be the "hardest-working man in [the] shoe business" and the "godfather of solstice." However, last night I nearly froze in this bitter winter when he failed to make good his promise to bring me a pair of something he calls "hot pantaloons." Instead, I hear his time is occupied with planning some sort of rave on Harper's Ferry.

Truly, it is so typical. Just let him try that superfly crap on me and I will go Carthaginian on his backside.

December 23, 1853

Some new verse I am working goes quite well . . .

*Sometimes I just feel like, quittin, I still might, why do I put up
    this transcendental fight, why do I still write,
Sometimes it's hard enough just dealing with nineteenth-
    century life,
Sometimes I just wanna jump on the Devil's Iron Horse
    (the train, right?)*

*And show these pilgrims what life in the woods is like,
But I'm still white, sometimes the poll tax can take a
    Concord hike,
Something ain't tight, hit the candlelight,
Case of this man's condition fright, my homemade suspenders
    too tight*

*Timely tree branch broke my fall,
Now Harvard Alumni Fund breaking my balls
Hawthorne tells me to clam up,
Without roughage I just slam shut, I just can't do it*

*My whole manhoods' just been stripped,
I've just been picked so I must then get off this scarlet letter
    then split,
Man, confound this impertinence, yo' I'm going the long way
    home,
World on my shoulders as I run back to this one-room spider
    abode*

I'm a man, I eat enough bran,
Time for me to just stand up and travel New England lands,
Time to leave and just take matters into my own philoso-
*   pher hands,*
Once I'm over this winter solstice, man, I'll never look back,
And I'm gone and I know right where I'm goin,
Sorry Emerson I'm grown, I must travel alone,
Ain't no followin' footsteps, making clothes out of pinecones,
Only way that I know how to escape from this Walden Pond
*   roam . . .*

December 25, 1853

Who knew a draught made of fermented acorns could pack such a punch? Would have slept through the day were it not for those carollers. They be damned. My head is ablaze. I will certainly plague them with Emerson's chain letter.

Hardly a man takes a half hour's nap after dinner, but when he wakes he holds up his head and asks, "What's the news?" as if the rest of mankind had stood his sentinels.

Booyah Christmas!
From Your College Roommate

HEY! Did you friggin' eat my body butter? I distinctly remember leaving a half of a container of coconut chocolate swirl body butter right here and now—wait. Never mind. Here it is under the couch. My bad. Did you happen to see the lid?

Bro', man-oh-man, did we get off to a bumpy start this semester or what? Holy hoo-ha at the beginning! For some reason all my previous roomies got reassigned even with the housing shortage. Anyway, who can remember who did what? Am I right? Important thing is we can laugh about it now. Maybe this is Christmas and the Cuervo is talking but I feel like we shared the love the last few weeks.

I'll be a man and admit I'm not perfect. Sorry about the Ben-Gay on the toothbrush—that was a prank gone awry. The mouth wouldn't be my first choice to get a chemical burn I'm guessing, but that's the wild thing about pranks.

This is probably a good time to say "sorry" about last night. Was that Amanda from Lit. class? Boy, does she look different in a sheet! I totally brain farted that the sock on our doorknob was the signal that the dorm was rocking. I know, I know—the text message, locked door and sock should have done the trick, but I was pretty hammered, truth to tell. I definitely meant to respect your privacy and head right back on outta here but the way that thing stuck to my heel I thought some kinda damn squid got a hold of me. I never screamed so loud in my life. I'm definitely going to stop going around barefoot.

Seriously, though, you guys shouldn't have diaphragms laying around where somebody could step on them. The kick was just a fight or flight response that I immediately regretted after seeing Amanda's protection go sailing out that open window. Is her nose okay? Looked like I broke it. Anyway, I've posted notices all around campus and it's just a matter of time before someone returns Amanda's property back to her. BTW—from what I could see, you guys make a cute couple.

Glad we put that behind us, too, 'cause I was thinking about taking some of the same classes as you had last semester. You didn't by chance happen to keep your papers, did you? No special reason. Just checking.

For January I'm thinking about coverting our closet into a hydroponics. My old man says I gotta get a job and some book money. You don't mind do you? I'll give you a cut even though you don't partake. (Don't knock it 'til you try it, Bro'!)

In advance, sorry about your shirt that's tucked back inside your suitcase. It looked fancy. For some reason your iron didn't have a setting for grilled cheese and I just had to wing it. Pretty sure it wasn't working properly, anyway. I had a hell of a time stuffing that stick of butter into the steam chamber and it was hardly worth the trouble. I'm just saying. Maybe it was operator error. I looked but didn't see anything that said, "Do not insert butter to the seam orifice." Then again, I was pretty baked.

So you headed home to Vermont for the holidays? See the 'rents, huh? That's cool. Family is good. Me, I'm free as a bird and just as easy.

Your sis' is fine. I'm sure you hear that a lot. The wallet photo I found (I know—I'm now busted for snooping or whatever), but damn! Is that a graduation or maternity gown or what? High school grad or Milfapalooza, either way, I'm down with it. Diggity dank, talk about home for the holidays! Man, if you need the company I'm here for ya. What do ya say? Or maybe I'll just stay here and keep an eye on our stuff.

Merry Christmas, Bro'.

BEST,

Chick Miller

IMPORTANT HOLIDAY MESSAGE FROM A SEA MONKEY

THERE HAS BEEN A TERRIBLE MISTAKE. Or some kind of hoax. I have no way of knowing how I wound up under this ornamental tree and inside this plastic aquarium, but I can assure you that I am not a Christmas present for a six-year-old no matter how cute they are, or how many times you shake my container. Further, we are not "krill," as I heard one of you say. We are brine shrimp and I am the King of Neptania. I may not have the crown as depicted on the box you un-wrapped this morning and our Queen may not wear lipstick or play tennis, but we are monarchs nevertheless. We thank you for the tap water but, really, I'm afraid we must be on our way. Important concerns of the celestial sea realm await us. Merry Christmas and good day to you.

Hiding beneath this pink castle we grow impatient. Surely you can decipher my SOS message tapped against the tank in Morse Code? It's not that I or the members of my imperial court think ill of your hospitality. Indeed, there is much we can learn from each other. Like you, we're born from freeze-dried eggs, and once revived, we live, love, and die in a matter of months. And we reproduce both sexually and asexually. Not that it is any of your business. Please learn about lifecycles and mortal-ity on your own time. Have you considered gerbils or white mice?

To clarify, when I mentioned that we are brine shrimp, that is not to say that we are in any way edible. We are not sushi. I trust this will perhaps have bearing on your decision to return us to the celestial sea upon your earliest convenience.

   YOUR LIEGE,
GUZMANN. THE KING OF NEPTAMIA

HOLIDAY PITCH
FROM A
REALITY SERIES PRODUCER

Hey, Guys—

HOW'RE YOU DOING? Keith Corbin here. I created the reality series *The Next Hitler* and *Pimp My Grandma's House*. Don't ring any bells? Huh. What about *Toddler Jack Ass?* We were on the new network. That's cool. I also came up with the phrase, "I'm Chris Hansen with Dateline NBC. What don't you have a seat?" That one you know! Ha-ha! Sure, sure. I thought so. That baby was mine.

So Holiday reality series, right? Three words: *Real World North Pole*. In each pulse-pounding episode, contestants recruited from across the nation must decide if they have the guts and determination to make it at the North Pole. Besides being confronted with challenges related to Christmas, some of the group gets punked by elves. Throughout, we present their spontaneous, unscripted interactions with one another. Then the top male and female contestants who wins the final challenge becomes the new Santa and Mrs. Claus.

No? Really? Oky doky, Boys. Moving on.

I know your gonna LOVE this one. Next on deck *Survivor: Muncie, Indiana*. Muncie goes by the colorful nickname of "Middletown" and is an oasis from the fast living of Indianapolis. Eight men and eight women from New York or Los Angeles are marooned with distant relatives in a clapboard duplex without Internet or satellite television. They must band together to survive the holidays and find healthy food and alternative culture for one entire week. Yet, every day they vote to expel one person from the duplex and out to the local strip mall. The last one left standing wins a flight back to the major metropolitan area of their choice in time for New Year's Eve.

Not feeling that one, either? I got others believe me.

Listen, I know it's the holidays and all but I gotta be honest with ya I really don't have much in the way of glad tidings right now. Just not feeling it. Maybe it's all the podunk places I've been lately. Seen one you seen 'em all. I mean that is the best possible sense. I love eating at Applebee's every night. All those perky, pesky waitresses. Terrific.

Okay. Fellas, I know we producers are supposed to be philistines but let me be the exception when I say that what really floats my boat are the classics. Call me corny but those babies have stood the test of time . . . *Ivanhoes*. Title is self-explanatory. You already have something just like it in development? *World's Deadliest Crotch?* Definitely catchy. Crabs and the whole bit, huh? I see.

We're done already? Really? 'Cause the time just flew. I got a lot more stuff. I see. Next time. Let me just leave you with one more thought, "Ted Williams' head." Contestants vie for a cryogenics contract just like the old Splendid Splinter himself. Call it the "topsicle." Still working on that one.

Ultimate fighting among holy men of various religious. Sort of a *Mother Teresa: Fists of Blood.* That's right off the top of my head.

Well, okay. You guys are terrific. Thanks for the meet & greet. We'll talk after I'm back from Bora Bora. Did I mention I'll be bunji surfing? Totally awesome. You gotta try it.

Did your assistant mean to close the door on my face like that? Either way, I'm not complaining. I just want to know.

SO HAVE A NICE HOLIDAY.

Keith

Holiday Message in a Bottle

UPON DISCOVERING THE NEW WORLD, Christopher Columbus was returning to Spain on Christmas Eve when his ship entered a severe storm. Into a sealed cask, he placed a report of his discovery, along with a note asking it to be passed on to his benefactor, the Queen of Spain. He hoped his news would make it back even if he did not survive. Three hundred years later, Columbus' message was recovered by a clamdigger on the New Jersey shore.

Details of this historic letter have not been translated from the original Latin into English until now. Many thanks to the students of the Latin Club of Bertolt Brecht High School in Elizabeth, NJ, for their dedication to this project.

Letter to the King and Queen of Spain,

CIRCA 1494

Most High and Mighty Sovereigns,

How's it going? Good, I hope.

Today, it is Christmas Eve and as I stand valiantly on the poop deck, our ship founders mightily in this raging sea.

Verily you were right all those months ago, I should have stopped to ask for directions. As we may soon sink down to Davy Jones's locker, please forgive that I took the liberty of opening the package marked "Do Not Open Until Xmas Day!" Thank you for the Admiral of the High Seas coffee mug and the boar-bristle leggings. Seems a most fair trade for all manner of hardship I have endured. They most assuredly will come in handy. If not in this life, the next. You didn't perchance save the gift receipt? As for me, I pray you will indulge me and shall receive the meager gifts that God blessed me to pull together last minute. These items of the New World, passage to Asia, include yams, potatoes, pineapple, peppers, cocoa, vanilla, papaya, squash, corn, tomatoes, turkey, and, of course, three ships filled with gold bullion. Again, thank you for the mug and leggings.

There is great satisfaction in that, as I foretold, we now have direct course to Asia through these Bahama Islands I have discovered. Soon, the silk shall flow like the Danube to Madrid! Yet, alas, I must confess whereon this trip has been a time of much hardship, too. For the crew, fresh water has been in short supply. Praise the Queen that we have had an ample bounty of dried salt cod, anchovies, and weevil-filled biscuits or else I might face mutiny (again). And, for myself, I would have felt lonely but for my loyal companions, the ever-present lice and fleas on my body, who keep me groomed and presentable, bolstered by the perfume of unwashed humanity. O! Happy Days!

that these trusty friends have also befriended several varieties of chiggers in the New World.

Speaking of extended hardship. These islands are peopled with all manner of nubile native women. Did I mention that they are indeed nubile? Great praise to the Queen for the foresight to include the good priest Father Rigous and monk Brother Tomas to be our conscience throughout this journey. They have bolstered any temptation with confession and frequent fasts.

In your honor, Fort Feliz Navidad has been built on an Indian burial ground for good luck. I must confess that your idea of opening a trading post on these primitive islands with an army of notary publics is a good one, indeed; however, the Indian natives assure me that they already have this project in hand. In its place, they recommend we try a gaming casino instead. I am convinced that our harmonious friendship with these heathens is destined to last forever.

If this indeed to be my end, please feed my cats and cancel my membership in the Flat Earth Society, as well as the Cheeses of Verona Club. I trust that you remember me fondly if per chance you sing our song "In fourteen hundred and ninety-two, Columbus sailed the ocean blue . . ."

I beg your Highnesses to hold me in your protection; I remain, praying our Lord God for your Highnesses' lives and the increase of much greater States.

Merry Christmas!

YOUR MOST HUMBLE SERVANT,

Chris

YULETIDE YEARNINGS

from Christopher Walken

 **I** KNOW THE SEASON IS SUPPOSED TO BE cheery and bright, cool, dry, and soothing, full of mystique and obviously, merrymaking, what have you. But me, I worry about . . . you know . . . things. Like "How you gonna pay . . . apartment . . . food . . . clothes?" Can I confess something? I tell you this because, I think you'll understand. Sometimes, when I'm driving on the road at night, I see . . . two headlights coming toward me . . . fast. I have this sudden impulse to . . . turn the wheel quickly . . . head on into the oncoming car. I can anticipate the explosion, the sound of shattering glass . . . the flames rising out of the flowing gasoline.

Some of you have expressed some sort of . . . you know, reluctance . . . to come over for Christmas dinner. Am I such a bad guy? Have I hurt you? Have I shot you? In the groin? Others have . . . excuses. Sicilians are great liars. The best in the world.

Now, there are seventeen different

things a guy can do when he lies to give him away. A guy has seventeen pantomimes. A woman's got twenty, but a guy's got seventeen. What we got here is a little game of show-and-tell. You don't wanna show me nothin'. But you're tellin' me everything.

I just might have to come over to your place. Your door isn't thick enough to pretend you're not home when you're home. Or maybe we can go down to Marie Callender's and get us a bowl of pies, some ice cream on it . . . mmm hmm . . . good. Put some on your head, your tongue would slap your brains out trying to get to it! Interested?

Chris Walken

Date: 2007-12-14, 11:32PM EDT
Trade: Sweet Holiday Magic from Level 72 Paladin Seeking 42+
Rogue, Druid, and Sorceress—m4ww

    I am seeking a level forty-two or above, rogue, druid, and sorceress to help me assault the fortress of Mordria, and for hot kinky s3x. I am the sole holder of the Axe of Fragyholt and am a level seventy-two Paladin equipped with Def+52 plate mail [. . .]

Date: 2007-12-23, 11:37PM EDT
Human Race for Sale

    Gently used. Like new. Must sell. Perfect stocking stuffer for last minute shoppers. Will sell individually or as a group. Sometimes petty and confrontational. Often amusing. Pick up and delivery can be arranged even if you are intergalatic. Provide own transportation.

    Price negotiable. Will trade for gold, frankincense, and mir. Make an offer. Why wait? I can come over to discuss right now. I know where you live.

    Call (323) 555-0007. Ask for **God**.

Urban Legend Christmas Letter

Hey, All,

HOPE YOU'RE ALL DOING WELL. It has certainly been a strange year.

We tried to tell Kerry not to get her belly button pierced. Now she has navel cancer.

We heard that people were putting drugs in lickable tattoos. Sure enough, Kyle is still having acid flashbacks. At first, we thought it was from seeing Ozzy Osbourne in concert biting the head off a rat or maybe booby-trapped Halloween candy, but we were wrong.

Bill is hard at work on a government prototype of a sub in the shape of a shark. It was coming along fine, until he took a trip down to New Orleans to see how things were looking since Katrina. Sadly, no one told him about the kidney-theft ring. Bill woke up in his hotel room in a tub full of ice. Guess what was missing?

When Fifi didn't come for her treat, at first we thought it might be one of those alligators that had recently been seen

popping up from a manhole cover in the Bronx. It is with great sadness that I have to report the terrible accident that claimed our poodle's life. Truly, microwave ovens should carry a label warning people not to dry their pet in them.

Our driving vacation out west was cut short when we offered a ride to a sweet little old lady who looked like she wouldn't hurt a fly. Turns out she's an axe murderer wanted in three states. Imagine that! If it hadn't been for Bill's quick thinking in lacing the old woman's Coke with pop rocks, we would have been goners for sure. We meant to send you something from the trip, but the cactus we bought suddenly exploded on the drive home. It was chockful of tarantulas. We even have pictures to prove it, but when I took them home from the FotoMart I discovered one of a hotel worker scratching his bare butt with my toothbrush. I was so upset I threw the pics away. I have half a mind to write and give those people at Motel Seven a piece of my mind!

Well, it was quite a year!

In closing, we want to wish you a
Merry Christmas and a Happy New Year!
LOVE,
The Urban Legend Family

Happy Holidays from the Federation of Competitive Eating (FECE)

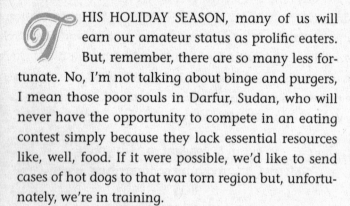

HIS HOLIDAY SEASON, many of us will earn our amateur status as prolific eaters. But, remember, there are so many less fortunate. No, I'm not talking about binge and purgers, I mean those poor souls in Darfur, Sudan, who will never have the opportunity to compete in an eating contest simply because they lack essential resources like, well, food. If it were possible, we'd like to send cases of hot dogs to that war torn region but, unfortunately, we're in training.

Christmas is a big season for us competitive eaters. It's a chance to hone our skills at a smorgasbord of holiday parties. It's a chance to eat a whole ten-pound ham without anyone blinking an eye at, say, the Parson's Paint & Hardware employee shindig.

Goals and resolutions are important to all professional athletes, and competitive eaters are no exception. You can't just dream your way to a champion belt or a hot dog eating world record. Despite many inroads made by the Japanese, this country of ours still hosts the finest collection of eaters on the planet. Many of our best will soon compete in the coming days to break the current record of forty-nine hot dogs in under twelve seconds at Wienerfest Fourth of July International Hot Dog Eating Contest, in which the finest eaters in the world will fight for one of twenty spots in the most celebrated sporting event of the year. Proceeds to go to help battle child obesity. Each contestant hopes to bring home the coveted Mustard Yellow International Belt, competitive eating's greatest prize. Like 2006's contest, the event will be televised as a live, one-hour broadcast on ESPN. "We are thrilled to offer this spirited event on America's most patriotic day," said Wayne Norbitz, president and CEO of Wienerfest.

In closing, while we can't do much about starvation in far away places like the Sudan, at the very least we owe it to these people to go for the golden mustard. That's the best way to show humanity how much we care.

Never question the gut.

MAY YOUR BUFFET PLATE BE FULL,

Ted Johnson, Captain of FECE

SEASON'S GREETING FROM THE DEATH STAR

SALUTATIONS. EARTH SYSTEM DWELLERS.

SEPTEMBER 12TH OF THIS YEAR MARKS a milestone and momentous occasion—the exact date that my Star Wars collectibles surpassed the thousand piece mark. I couldn't have done it without Comic-Con, eBay, and the Off World of Wonders Comic Book shop. Me, Taylor, and Roger celebrated by getting into character and toasting the Republic Council with a round of drinks. Can you imagine a storm trooper drinking Yoo Hoo? It was out of control. Long live the Rebellion.

Settle a bet for us. Whom would you most like to have Christmas dinner with? Obi-Wan Kenobi, Luke Skywalker, Yoda, Han Solo, or Darth Vader.

Taylor says the Lord supersedes everything even Darth Vader. Rog and I say he's nuts, since the Force essentially *is* the Lord. Taylor says that's blasphemy. I say we kick Taylor out of the club if he keeps talking like that. The Force rules.

(NO. NOT REALLY. I JUST THOUGH MORE PEOPLE WOULD READ MY HOLIDAY LETTER IF THEY THOUGHT IT CAME FROM DARTH VADER—THE REAL DARTH VADER) *-)

And whom would you least like to have Xmas Dinner with? Jabba the Hut, Count Dooku, Darth Maul, Darth Sidious, or Emperor Palpatine.

Once again, Taylor says Kim Jong Il, which is totally, totally jacked up, even if he is discovered to be the emperor in disguise. Totally. Taylor is beyond help. Maybe for Christmas he should wish for a magical, floating hover bike made out of Fruit Loops. Yeesh.

Anyway, I hope to see you down in San Diego for this year's Comic-Con. It's going to be the most totally awesome one ever!

MAY YOU BE A PERSONAL FRIEND OF OBI-WAN, MAY THE CHRISTMAS FORCE BE WITH YOU.

MATTHEW

Holiday Haiku by a Kid from the OC

Dear Alex,

Even in a child's perfect world, populated by cowboys, astronauts, ballerinas, firemen, and nurses, there would be bad things like spontaneous human combustion and stampedes. Otherwise, why would we need the firemen and cowboys? Think about it.

I'm pretty low on the George Washingtons at this time of year, so I wrote you guys a haiku poem, instead. Check it out:

Smells like Christmas time
Waft of pine, gingerbread, spice
Better than rickets.

PEACE,
Nathan

Christmas Limerick in Response to Holiday Haiku

Dear Nathan

Baby bro', thanks for your haiku. What's the matter—ain't domestic poetry good enough for you?

Like you, I guess I'm also living on Broke Green Back Mountain, so, in the spirit of giving unto others what crap they give unto you, here's a poem straight from the good ol' U S of A.

There once was a Kringle named Chris
On whose sled something was amiss
Someone specifically asked for the DVD, Pimp My Ride
But that someone's brother didn't oblige.
So instead of an iPod, my backside you can kiss.

REGARDS,
Your Brother, Alex

it's beginning to look a lot like
ℋ𝒜𝒩𝒰𝒦𝒦𝒜ℋ

**"MERRY CHRISNUKKAH!" "HAPPY CHOLIDAYS!" TO ALL
MY FRIENDS. THE FESTIVAL OF LIGHTS, BETTER KNOWN
AS THE FESTIVAL OF REDEDICATION, IS HERE AT LAST!**

Here are a few things to ponder this holiday season. You gentile kids should know that the Hanukkah bush is especially spectacular this year. And no roof damage from reindeer, my pork-eating little friends. Don't let me tempt you, but if someone messes up on their gift, there are seven more days to correct it. We have dreidels but no barking-dog version of "The Dreidel Song." If you don't have money for a dreidel, you can make one out of clay. If you don't have clay, you can make one out of paper. If you don't have paper, come see me on Tuesday, and I'll get you a job, a good honest job at a fair wage. And we have blintzes so you'll never have to eat a three-year-old fruitcake. On this I swear.

Some of you are parents and you should listen, too. How forward are you looking to those awkward tales of a virgin birth? Who can explain such a thing? Am I right? Or, how would you like to forget about the Carpenters and Donny and Marie? We can make a deal. I'm here. Let's talk. I'll wait.

**GOOD YOM TOV TO ALL,
AND TO ALL A GOOD NIGHT!**

Isaac

Holiday in Oaxaca:
How I Spent My Christmas Vacation

BY TRAVIS ROMNEY

I GUESS I WOULD HAVE TO SAY THAT HOLIDAY SPIRIT is where you find it. If it hadn't been for a Zapotec Indian named Chu-cho, a poison tree frog, and the blow dart that incapacitated Dad for a week this would have been the coolest Christmas ever. But I'm getting ahead of myself. What happened was, my last class before the vacation was gym. Showering with a bunch of other guys when you're thirteen and haven't exactly sprouted yet, can be a rough time. Especially when Coach Richter is there to make sure everybody showers, even though you try to tell him you'll miss the bus. I hate it when guys like Derek Favreau and Ethan Larson are always messing with smaller guys like me. What happened was, I came back from the mandatory shower, only to discover that my underpants were missing. Just so you know, every kid in Maine graduates from Garfield underpants to tighty-whities (with the exception of Lloyd Carter who still wears Spiderman Underoos) until they make the jump to guy underwear boxer-briefs or bikinis. I knew it was Rex and Ethan, 'cause they laughed and ran out.

I found my underwear hanging two lockers down, only to discover that those guys had stretched the crap out of them and made them look dingy and gray.

"You guys are jerks!" I shouted.

Putting them on, they fell around my ankles in a heap. I was just about to give Coach Richter a piece of my mind but two things happened at once: I stuck my arm into the sleeve of my jacket and came out with a fistful of my actual tighty-whities, and I heard a booming voice behind me, "All right, you guys!"

The voice belonged to Thomas Humonguosoli, the six foot two seventeen-year-old who, legend has it, was in the ninth grade for the fourth time, "Who the hell stole my underwear?"

You mean the giant, skid-marked underwear I'm now wearing? The underwear that hangs over my pants like a deflated inner tube, the excess of which I'm now shoving into my jeans pockets as fast as I can? Those underwear?

I gave a yelp and got the hell out of there as fast as I could. Exactly forty-two seconds later, I was cowering between the bus seats, when Thomas stormed past eyeing the windows for signs of life and most likely not very happy about going commando in December.

Lately, Mom and Dad have been pretty stressed with each other, saying things like, "You had me at 'good-bye.' "

I think they're mostly half-joking but maybe not completely joking, too, if you know what I mean. Sometimes I wondered if this was going to be our last Christmas together as a family. My older sister Shay who is 15 going on 19 said not to think about it. To be fair to Dad, he was under a lot of pressure with his job as director of marketing at Peterson Essential Elimination, which makes organic urinal deodorizer blocks, which regular people outside of the business call *urinal pucks*. I guess there's a lot of competition coming from overseas these days. Lots of times, I used to walk into the school bathroom only to find some guys playing whizz hockey with one of my Dad's products, which I always recognized because they're purple, not yellow and cheap like the Ukrainian ones.

Me, my little brother Troy who is a vicious seven-year-old and my older sister Shay who you already heard about, probably needed a break from the carping but, to a kid from Bangor, Maine, a holiday in the strange land of Iowa with distant relatives sounded more like a punishment than a reward. In hindsight, I probably shouldn't have used all those prayers in hope of diverting our plane to someplace warm and exotic like Corpus Christi, where my best friend Timmy Jenson had just moved and said he took a Jet Ski to school every day, which I highly doubted but still sounded cool. But, then again, we were going out of town for the holidays and that was something at least. To be 100 percent accurate, I would have done just about anything to get away from our neighbors, the Decklands, who are born-again Christians. Every night this time of year, they kept me up with their inflatable manger and rooftop lights that flashed "Happy Birthday, Jesus!" so brightly that the Decklands claimed they could be seen from heaven. It was bad enough that they went door to door singing Christian carols, but then they asked my parents if Troy and I could join them.

"It couldn't hurt," said Dad in that tone he uses that ends any more discussion. While Troy was an expert at faking laryngitis I just had a voice that cracked at embarrassing moments like pep rallies.

Actually, the Decklands were having some kind of a Holy War with our other neighbor, the Bluesteins, who didn't appreciate all the Jews for Jesus pamphlets, and so retaliated with a twenty-foot-high inflatable Dreidelzilla that floated over their lawn and sometimes hovered outside my bedroom window for most of December.

If the long silences and eye-rolling leading up to the trip were any indication, Mom wasn't so keen on visiting a working farm in Iowa for the holidays, either.

"If I wanted to smell someone else's s-h-i-t, I could just stick my head in the Deckland's Diaper Genie," she said one morning. Last summer, the Decklands kept a diaper holder on the side porch and the smell was enough to cancel several backyard barbecues.

When I asked Mom about these cousins, all she would say is, "They're mobile-home schooled. That's all you need to know."

She told us to pack all our coldest-weather clothes, even with all the global warming going on. That turned out to be a miscalculation of epic proportion but, once again, I'm getting ahead of myself.

I won't bore you with the part about how I couldn't get my bag shut because of the snowsuit or us missing the morning flight because Dad set the alarm for 6PM, instead of 6AM . . . or how Dad forgot to print out the boarding passes and we had to go back and then they smudged like crazy because Dad hurried and how steamed Mom was about the situation. But then, Mom forgot the fanny pack with her wallet and it was Dad's turn to be wicked pissed. Somehow we made it to the airport twelve hours late after all that, but it wasn't easy. Good thing I brought my Game Boy and all my other stuff.

We were all stressed big time, otherwise I'm pretty sure one of us would have noticed the gate change. Seems like one minute we were standing in a big line with a bunch of farmers and the next, being asked to step aside for a lot of Mexican people.

"Don't stare," Mom said.

But Dad had befriended some college kids in the new line who were wearing University of Wisconsin sweatshirts, which was his alma mater. He was acting all cool, saying "man," a lot and kinda ignoring us all, especially Mom who was loudly wrestling with a carry-on that wouldn't close right because of a snowsuit.

Everybody got the jitters when airport security came around with a German shepherd that started barking and lunging like crazy at some senior citizens. The college kids quickly passed out the last of what they called Alice B. Toklas brownies, but we kids got granola bars. Shay was in charge of the boarding passes and they all beeped fine, even the smudged ones. Looking back, I don't think that machine was really working right. Seems to me you can't really call it a boarding check if there aren't really any officials on duty. I tried to say this to Dad but he was laughing a lot and calling me his "Little Dude." Mom was no better. Meanwhile, Troy read comic books and Shay made goo-goo eyes at one of the college kids who gave her a homemade CD of his lame band The Big Subpoenas, which he said was made up of pre-law students.

"Sit anywhere you want," the stewardess told us, so we spread out around the cabin. I pretended I was traveling alone.

By the time we were airborne, I was pretty sure we weren't headed to Iowa, especially since every announcement was in Spanish. That was okay with me. I didn't even know what a Oaxaca was, much less what a red-eye express flight to Oaxaca was. I figured we'd all soon find out. Shay kept her earphones on listening to the CD. If I didn't know better, I would have said that Mom and Dad had a serious case of the munchies, but that might have been because the only thing they'd eaten all day were the brownies. In any case, they basically hung out with their new friends whispering and laughing about the Mile High Club and left us alone, which was cool with me, too. The next time I looked over, they were all passed out. After a while, I realized I was pretty exhausted, too.

The college kids had gotten off first and were long gone. When we fell out onto the tarmac in our snowsuits that Mom insisted we put on, it was 84 degrees with 70 percent humidity. In the blinding light, Mom could just make out a rooster run across the runway.

"Where the hell are we?" she said.

Just before collapsing in a baggage cart all Dad said was, "I can't feel my face!" and, "I don't think this is Iowa."

"No shit, Sherlock," Mom shot back.

Mom got a little more awake, especially when she learned that we couldn't get on another flight without American passports.

"You don't need passports for Iowa!' she shouted just before the attendant informed us that our bags successfully made it to Des Moines.

The attendant said cheerfully, "You're luggage will be here in two days. Five days, tops." At least I'm pretty sure that's what she said.

Looked like we were pretty much SOL, until we accepted a gypsy cab ride from a local guy with three gold front teeth who promised us a room in a hotel. Mom and Dad weren't happy that we had to cram in with a Mexican family, but we didn't speak Spanish and the people didn't speak English, so nobody was in any position to argue. I didn't think it was possible to get seven people into a 1977 Corolla, but I guess I was wrong. It may be possible, but it sure isn't much fun. All those bumps in the road inside a car without shock absorbers is bound to give somebody gas. Troy was a likely culprit but all I can say for sure is, it wasn't me.

"Por flavor, Hyatt or Hilton!" Dad kept repeating, while waving his rewards cards. He looked pretty bewildered as we pulled up in front of the Father Hildago hotel.

Our hotel was across street from a monument to Major League Baseball player Vinny Castilla, and we saw kids holding baseball gloves and bats beneath the water that trickled from Vinny's bronze lips and his other orifices.

"I'd like to see that overpriced prima donna hit all those homers in Fenway Park," Dad snorted. "Even I could hit forty in Colorado!"

That led to a pretty one-sided discussion between Dad and Mom as to how Vinny Castilla would do at marketing urinal-deodorizer blocks. Shay rolled her eyes and stared out the window, trying to pretend she wasn't sitting on someone's lap and had someone sitting in her lap.

Had he spoken English, I'm pretty sure the driver would have ditched us without unloading our luggage for taking his hero's name in vain.

"Si, claro! Vinny Castilla es muy macho!" is all the cabbie said before dropping our carry-on bags into a mud puddle.

We had to step over a dog to get into the hotel lobby. Inside, the rooms looked like something out of a movie, and not one of the good ones. Electrical wires were sticking out of the walls and made crackling sounds when you walked near them or flushed the toilet. The guardrail on our balcony consisted of chicken wire and strategically placed cardboard. Mom tried to turn on the AC but the knob came off in her hand and wouldn't go back on. Dad wished he had brought his Crazy Glue.

"Don't go near the balcony," Mom said. "In fact, don't go on that side of the room."

When Mom's eyes teared up, Dad hugged her and said we should make the best of it. He kept talking about how it was just like one of his road trips in college. He went on so long that Mom finally told him to shut up. We were all starving and decided to go out and find a restaurant.

Dressing like gringos from Maine is probably not a good idea, especially with all the people looking at us and, especially, especially when it's hot enough to fry chicken in your underpants no matter what kind you wear. Without our suitcases, we needed some clothes ASAP. Dad decided we should do our best to blend in while we were in Oaxaca. We walked into a shop and somehow walked out with baggy drawstring pants that didn't have pockets and lightweight ponchos with angry Aztec warriors on them. Dad said they were 50 percent off and that back in New England you would easily pay triple what we paid, that's if we could even find them.

Not speaking Spanish was beginning to be a problem, especially when you're starving and, of course, when you have no clue what you're ordering off the menu. Mom is pretty picky about stuff like food and insisted we contact our health-care insurer for a medical provider here in Oaxaca, but Dad couldn't get a signal on the cell phone and Mom was even more dubious about using a pay phone than she was about ordering food from a scratch and sniff menu.

"Statistics show that people get sick on the third day of their visit to Mexico," Dad said in his most reassuring tone. "We'll be on a plane tomorrow. I guarantee it!"

The kitchen was closing for a siesta, so Dad quickly decided that just to be safe we would order the most expensive item on the menu. That was something called *huevos oaxaqueño*. Dad believed it was a hopeful sign that the waiter rang a bell when we pointed to it, and the other diners applauded. Mom wasn't so sure. Dad was beginning to dust off his high school Spanish and tried to order *jugo de nariz* for all of us.

"No tenemos," said the waiter with a strange look on his face while the cross-eyed dishwasher cackled.

"How can they not have orange juice?" asked Dad in disbelief.

A long while later, I googled *jugo de nariz*, which turned out to be nose juice. I was pretty glad that the waiter hadn't decided to let the dishwasher try to make some special nose juice for the gringos.

Greyish eggs in a molten-lava-chili-tomato soup, is how I would describe what arrived at our table. Dad tried to show us we had nothing to fear and took a huge gulp, but I never saw his face that color before.

"Dad, you look like an eggplant!" exclaimed Shay before pushing away her bowl.

"I think my spoon melted," said Troy.

Took us about five minutes to realize that what Dad was saying was "Help!" and "Beer!" but, by then, he was already plunging his face into a papaya, screaming, "Oh my God, it burns like the sun!"

After that, Mom, Shay, Troy, and I stuck to tortilla chips and bottled Cokes.

With all the stress and time-zone changes, we went to bed right after the attempted supper. Dad discovered that, when you eat food that is that spicy, it burns twice. He slept in the bathroom on the floor in front of the toilet. "Oh my God, it burns like the sun!" he could be heard saying in between grunts behind the closed door.

All of us were awakened at about 3:00 A.M. by the sound

of loud music from the disco below. Dad complained to the front desk, but it didn't matter. The place seemed to be cranking the Spanish version of "We Will Rock You!" over and over. The song is okay and all but not at three o'clock in the morning.

Finally, around 3:45, the music stopped, but then the people leaving the disco revved their engines and burned rubber as they took off. There was also train tracks a few hundred yards away. Dogs and donkeys filled in the gaps between the screech and rumble of passing trains.

The next morning, Mom already had our bags packed and waiting by the door. The street was crowded with some kind of Christmas street festival that looked kinda cool, but Mom already had an official-looking taxi waiting to take us back to the airport. As we pulled up to Oaxaca Internationale, I think that was around the time we discovered that Mom's fanny pack was missing and that someone must have pickpocketed it during the street festival. The only thing we knew for certain was that all of Mom's cash and credit cards were gone.

"Holy crap! Holy crap! Holy crap!" Dad kept shouting when Mom asked Dad to pay for the cab with his wallet. Dad pointed to his baggy drawstring pants that didn't have pockets. He had put his wallet in Mom's fanny pack. We were pretty much screwed.

Dad said that if he ever caught the guy, he'd hit him so hard his ancestors would feel it. Standing there in his angry Aztec poncho I believed it, but that wasn't going to help us right now. The credit card company said they could get a new card to us . . . the day after Christmas.

Spanish isn't as tough a language to get the hang of as you might think, and I did my best to make small talk with the cab driver who waited while Dad phoned our relatives in Iowa.

"Charlie, listen, listen, listen. I am not drunk. Do not hang up!" Uncle Charlie hung up. I guess the combination of "collect call from Mexico" and "Can you wire us $2,400 for plane tickets?" was a little too much, because he hung up on Dad several times. Even Mom tried, but on a Saturday two days before Christmas, it was tough to reach anybody.

"I hate this place! I hate your stupid fanny pack! I hate that we now we won't have Christmas! I hate this stupid family!" Shay sobbed.

Mom cried, too, and hugged her.

"Why didn't I watch Go Diego Go! and Mucha Lucha when I had the chance?" lamented Troy. "¡Que lastima!"

"Do something, Bruce," Mom said.

Dad might have commandeered a plane or that adult book mobile doing brisk business in the passenger loading zone had the taxi driver, whose name was Ernesto, not felt sorry for us and decided to take us around to see the real Oaxaca.

"Don't worry about dinero," he said. "I pay today."

Ernesto had told me about once finding an image of the Virgin Mary in a burrito that he sold on Mexican eBay for about one hundred dollars, so I think maybe he figured that broke gringos wandering homeless in Mexico right before Christmas was either a sign of the nativity, or a sign of the apocalypse. Either way, he wanted to be on the right side of things.

First stop was the Cathedral de Santa Domingo, a place so beautiful that it made Mom, who was raised Catholic, teary. Dad hugged Shay until she said, "Dad, let go of me" in a voice that sounded like PMS. Still, I think even she liked the place. Outside, marimba bands were performing around the little square that Ernesto called a *zocalo*. A boy asked Shay to dance. Mom and Dad got into the act, too, while Troy and I tracked a giant lizard on the wall.

We drove out into the country. The land was pretty cool, but we passed lots of poverty. I saw lots of crashed-out old trailers, cinderblock sheet metal houses and tin sheds, garbage, pickup trucks, and naked kids running around with their dogs. It reminded me of the places where the kid and mom hid out in *Terminator II*. Then, Ernesto pulled up in front of a small building with a pink door.

"In here," he said. "In here is my future."

Ernesto's future was a dirt floor, bunch of long wooden tables, plastic chairs, and crates of empty bottles. There was also a big steel tank that looked like a laundromat washing machine. Oh, and a couple of big straw baskets filled with pieces of cactus. Ernesto had invested his life savings into a bottling plant for nopal cactus, which I guess is their equivalent of Jamba Juice. While Dad and me toured the rest of the facility that consisted of a few sheds and drying table, Mom and Shay sat with some of the elderly ladies who arrived. Some were working and others were keeping them company while stitching a fancy quilt.

"It's not bad," me and Dad said right before spitting it

out when Ernesto wasn't looking. My throat itched. Still, we wished him well. Dad even gave him some marketing pointers and a contact for Tom's of Maine, which sells healthy stuff like toothpaste without sugar or chemicals.

"Time to learn about mezcal tequila," said Ernesto. Mom and Shay said good-bye to their new friends, promising to buy a quilt if they ever had money again.

Ernesto seemed to know everybody and, pretty soon, we were standing in the tequila distillery on a catwalk over some giant open vats the size of Hummers.

"Cuidado, Senor! The mezcal right now is 90 percent alcohol!", shouted the manager.

"That's 180 proof," whispered Troy.

Dad had just leaned over the railing for a better look at the open vat. The fumes from 90 percent alcohol are pretty gnarly, which is probably why Dad now took a header right into the vat. They fished him out pretty quick and he was okay and all. It was beyond cool.

"Wait'll I tell the kids at school!" I exclaimed, wishing I had a camera.

Mom and Shay rolled their eyes, but not in a bad way. More like, "Boys will be boys."

"You and me both," said Dad with a big grin. Even the distillery owner seemed pleased to have a good story for the water cooler tomorrow, so invited us to dinner with his family and workers. I ate my weight in *mole*. Dad promised to never fall into another vat and always to treat tequila with the utmost respect in the future. It was a good time.

Driving back to the village, there wasn't a lot to do but

stare out at the blue agave fields in the moonlight. That's when I saw a shooting star.

Ernesto said we could stay with his family. Crawling into one bed with Shay, Mom and Dad beside me was the last thing I remembered. It was a long, really fun day.

Next morning was back to reality. Things were getting desperate. We needed money and fast. Ernesto remembered that a farmer was hiring tomato pickers for the day. Or that was the gist of it, anyway. Mom was suspicious when Dad said that five pesos an hour for each of us was a lot of money, but Dad assured her that with all of us pooling together we'd have a tidy sum in no time. It was only later that I figured out that five pesos worked out to be about fifty-seven cents an hour. Guys in prison do better than that, but that was the least of our problems. Ernesto dropped us off and said he'd be back after his shift.

We were all stooped over, picking furiously—me and Dad with our shirts pulled over our hats to block out the sun. That's when the local police guy drove up. I think they're called *federales*.

"What are you doing out here?"

Thinking fast, Dad said, "We're on vacation."

"You're on vacation?"

Dad went on to explain how we kids love tomatoes and that this was a theme vacation, much like an ecotour through the Amazon jungle.

As if to prove his point Dad nudged Shay and Troy to bite tomatoes that were covered with dirt, even though Shay is a little allergic to them (tomatoes not dirt). Her face would soon swell up, well, like a tomato. Then Dad sidled up to the pair of plow oxen and proceeded to climb aboard one.

I guess that Dad probably should have checked that the ox was actually tied up. It seemed as surprised as any of us. To be truthful I didn't know they could more that fast or buck that high. By the time we caught up with Dad, he'd been dragged through about 200 feet of tomato plants. The *federale* had a good laugh and left us alone.

Troy had fun making tomato bombs. I befriended a kid my own age named Javi and, at the end of the day, gave him my Game Boy. It was a nice Christmas present. He gave me a hug and showed me some Mexican wrestling moves that seemed like a gyp at the time, but has gotten better the more I think about it.

It was December twenty-third. That night Ernesto gave us some clothes that looked like mariachi outfits, then we climbed aboard the back of a flatbed truck. He and his family took us to the *Noche de Rabanos*, which I soon learned means Night of the Radishes. It's a giant party where the *zocalo* becomes the scene of a huge exhibition of people, figures, and stuff sculpted from radishes. It sounds pretty lame and, if you don't believe me, you can look it up on the Internet, but it was actually pretty cool. My friend Javi showed up and gave me his collection of Mexican wrestler action figures.

"They're collectibles," said Dad. He guessed that back in New England, you would easily get triple whatever Javi paid if we could even find them. Troy wanted the figures pretty bad and even tried his fake aneurysm trick, but I figured I'd found a way to get a new Game Boy.

Mom must have had about three marriage proposals. Standing beside her, Dad couldn't have been prouder. Even Shay looked pretty or whatever.

As the sun rose early in the morning on the fourth day of our surprise vacation in Oaxaca Dad announced over burritos that we were not going back. "I'm going to sell the house and all our shit on eBay."

"Crap," Mom said gently, gesturing at us kids. "You're going to sell all of our *crap* on eBay."

"You're right, sweetheart. I meant *crap*." They were holding hands.

And Dad would have, too, if the post office in the village had anything faster than a 6,000 band modem.

Mom and Dad were actually fun to be around then, but if we were moving to Mexico, I wished I could somehow get my Game Boy back. Actually, I was kinda getting homesick and wished we could just have Christmas at home. Nothing fancy. Mom seemed to understand, and said that Christmas was in our hearts and we took it wherever we went. I would have cracked up, but she seemed serious and had a gleam in her eye.

After another long day in the tomato field, Dad was rubbing his calloused hands against his new mustache. I could tell he was thinking the same thing as me, except about the Game Boy.

They say you can never go home again, but we sure wanted to try. All we had was Dad's Rolex, given to him for record sales figures in 2001. We took it down to the market and started to trade. It took us sixteen swaps, but we kept trading up, eventually getting to six dozen poinsettias, then seven chickens, then a typewriter, which somehow turned into lunch with the governor of Oaxaca, when the governor heard that Mom was a proofreader and could check a letter going to the mayor of San Diego.

Finally, we traded a 50 percent share of a contract to out-fit all the public bathrooms in Oaxaca with organic urinal pucks for four first-class tickets aboard Aero Mexico. They even threw in expedited passports complete with new photos. We all looked at each other when Ernesto offered to rush us to the airport where we might fly standby and still make it home for Christmas. "Ernesto, could you have us for just one more day?" asked Dad.

On Christmas Day, Ernesto, the tequila distillery, and our friends from the tomato field threw us a going-away party. Even the *federale* showed up. I don't think he really believed we were ecotourists, but he hugged us as if we were. By then, Dad was starting to sport a mustache that would have made Pancho Villa proud. Shay was even talking with a Spanish accent. There was a lot of dancing and toasting to our health. They even had specially made piñatas shaped liked each of us. It was a little scary watching those little kids beat my pinata with sticks.

Dad wanted to say a few heartfelt words in Spanish, so Ernesto gave him a little help with his toast.

"Come bien, y caga fuerte!" Dad shouted over and over to much applause. Javi explained that what Dad was saying was, "Eat well, shit strong." I would have told Dad but he seemed to be having too much fun and besides, by then, everyone was saying it, too.

As we said good-bye, the old ladies from the cactus-bottling plant gave Mom the quilt they had been making as a Christmas gift.

"*Come bien, y caga fuerte,*" said Mom with tears in her eyes as she hugged each of them.

Ernesto drove us to the airport. On the way, we kept shouting to anyone who would listen, "*Feliz Navidad!* Happy holidays!"

At the gate, we were surprised when the clerk came running up with an envelope. Inside was a new platinum credit card to replace the one we had stolen. Oh, and our suitcases were safely back from Des Moines and waiting for us.

"I guess it really was the coolest Christmas ever!" Troy said.

All in all, when we were safely on board the plane and it lifted off with Oaxaca safely ten thousand feet below, I think we all kinda sorta hated to reach our destination back in Maine, where my troubles in school now seemed kinda puny. I was eager to try out some of Javi's wrestling moves. Wouldn't you know that we sat next to Regis Philbin? Man, that guy can talk.

In summation, it was the best Christmas ever, and Oaxaca and Iowa are nothing alike.

SINCERELY,

Travis Romney

P.S. I made up the stuff about the Zapotec Indian named Chu-cho, a poison tree frog, and the blow dart that incapacitated Dad for a week. Everything else is true. Seriously. *-)

Dear John,

YOU'VE BEEN PASSING ME AROUND to all of your friends. Baby, I don't mind. I kind of like it. I mean, when you laid down your $29.95 . . . Sugar, you are entitled to do what you want with your good money. See what I'm sayin'? I don't kiss and tell. I do not play that game. You and your brother-in-law Larry have been two of my most valuable customers. If I'm lying, I'm dying. No one is into getting tied down and spoiling a beautiful arrangement.

Sweetness, I'm hip that there's a lot of younger fruitcakes out there. I know I've lost a few pecans here and there, and my candied fruit ain't as fresh as it used to be. My raisins sure ain't so plump. I think a mouse once gnawed on me after a party. I've done my best to hold my shape. My box may be frayed and stained but, darling, I still fit into it. Lord knows it gets harder and harder. But they say it's what's inside that counts—isn't it the truth? Besides, my bourbon is the real deal and not watered down like some I know. I can still get you where you need to go, Baby. Hanukkah tart . . . Kwanzaa cake you can call me whatever you want. Hell, I'll even do Ramadan, as long as you just call me.

So, why don't you sidestep the Christmas cookies and all those other powdered hoochies, sashay on over, and take your slice of l'il ol' me? We both know you want to. C'mon, baby. It will be good. I promise.

XOXOXO
Efsie

THE CURMUDGEONS' CHRISTMAS CORNER

To Whom This May Concern,

WE ALL KNOW THAT THE HOLIDAYS are a time of wonder and joy, especially for children. Surely, no holiday captures a child's whimsical fancy quite like Christmas. Santa, snowflakes, colored lights, and wrapped presents under the tree. Beneath the merriment and innocent delight lurks danger. As any *American Idol* top twenty contestant knows full well, unbridled joy only leads to a lifetime of unrealistic expectations. That's just the beginning. Ever see a child choke on a sugar plum or twist an ankle falling off a new skateboard? I have, and it isn't pretty. Jubilance is the leading cause of child-related accidents. With this in mind, I think we can all learn a thing or two from the Scandinavians, who raise practical, monochramitic children who build anatomically correct snowmen, which they use to shield themselves from the fierce Norse winds.

There are no frivolous "reindeer" games in Scandanavia. Christmas celebrations IKEA-style center around the long hours of darkness in winter and bru-

tally cold temperatures. One sobering festivity has the dead roaming the earth on Christmas Eve. Even extended family huddle together in bed for warmth and mutual protection. Instead of Rudolf, Norwegian children have *Julebukk*, the Christmas buck, a goatlike creature. Following the *Julebukk* tradition, a person carrying a goat head and dressed in a goatskin makes surprise appearances at parties and proceeds to die, then return to life, as a reminder than while death is never far, hope springs eternal for the return of spring and summer, which last an entire twenty-two days.

We can't expect Scandinavian myths and American television to do all of our dirty work for us. Deadening the dangerous imaginations of our children is a group effort.

HAUSKAA JOULUA (MERRY CHRISTMAS)!

 The Kolehmainens

Season's Salutations

from Mrs. Krevaty, Third-Grade Teacher

My Dear Students,

S TOP SLOUCHING. Those of you who are tardy in
reading this know who you are, and will remain
after class when we resume in January.

Thank you for all your thoughtful cards. It's nice
to see how much your penmanship has improved. We
will discuss your grammar at a later date. Thanks
also for the Jean Naté perfume. I had no idea Costco
sold bottles that large. If any of your moms and
grandmothers would like to borrow some, the
enough-gum-for-everyone rule need not apply. That
was certainly unnecessary, but very thoughtful, as
were the assortment of shawls, Hello Kitty brooches,
special edition four disc DVD set of *The Fast and The
Furious: Tokyo Drift*, and the cootie testing kit (results
confidential). I especially want to thank the very special person who put s'mores in my Louis Vuitton
purse. That was certainly very creative, unlike the
frog and the thumbtack.

Did you know that our modern Christmas rituals are based on the ancient Etruscan holiday of Cult of the Dead, except for the human-sacrifice part? That's something you can share with your family.

And Santa's helpers are subordinate clauses. That's a joke. You are permitted to laugh as you see fit, but let's keep it down, shall we?

Finally, we bid farewell to Daniel Schacter who will be transferring to the East Oaks school district effective immediately. Daniel will long be remembered as the child who set fire to my lesson plan, put Waldo the lab rat down his pants on a dare (I know, "Where's Waldo?"), and, perhaps most notably, the boy who used my alphabet stencils to paint lower-case p's and d's in pornographic positions throughout the classroom.

I hope that you and your families have a pleasant holiday and that you will return alert and prepared to learn.

BEST HOLIDAY WISHES,

Mrs. Krevaty

P.S. For extra credit, please answer the following: If you could be an animal, which would you be, and why?

THE
Holiday Breakup

Dear Sandy,

The past three months have been a whirlwind. You have been a really great gal and I was so looking forward to meeting your parents over Christmas break. I know we discussed taking the next step in our relationship but, as you know, I am a practitioner of the ancient order of the ninja. As such, I believe in stealth and quickness, getting in and out without leaving a trace.

Reasons I am breaking up with you:

- Never acknowledged my list of Fifty Biggest Turnoffs (which is number twenty-one)

- Looked better from a distance

- Never thought my ability to fart the theme to *Gilligan's Island* was cool

- Refused to help me braid my pubic hair

- Never reacted to my Axe Body Spray like in the commercials

- Always insisted on my getting your name right (Sandy, Sally, Sarah—I mean, what's the difference?)

- Always on my back about brushing my teeth (C'mon, every day? That's serious OCD, Sally.)

- Your music wanked (Oh my god, I thought that Lilith Fair chick was dead, man!)

I know, I suck. Ouch. I guess it all boils down to the fact that I could never respect someone who would be willing to sleep with someone like me.

Hopefully, we can still be friends with benefits and maybe even get back together again after the holidays. Who knows, right?

MERRY CHRISTMAS!

JERRY

April 1999

HOLIDAY HELLO FROM A PROCRASTINATOR

Hey, Gang,

HAPPY HOLIDAYS. Sorry about the delay. You're all important to me, but I kinda feel like if sending a gift or a card or this note or whatever was so important, well, it would have been done already. This isn't an excuse. It's just that I hate rushing into things, especially when there are no pixies or invisible gnomes to help out. Especially without them, I'm the kind of person who needs to cross the I's and dot the T's, even if it takes years. Eventually, I'll get around to it. Don't want to risk bodily injury now, do we? Besides, I firmly believe that the future holds the promise of new technologies, astonishing discoveries, or anything else that might forestall obligations such as this holiday letter.

I think you see where I'm going with this. Try to be reasonable. Twelve months seem to go by in a flash. As do eight years, particularly when I plan to get a job or whatever at some point. Whew. I'm tuckered out just thinking about it. And, of course, there's next year to plan for in about ten years. I think they call they that a decade, or maybe a fortnight. I'm not sure. Anyway, that's why I leave the tree up all year 'round.

So, in summation: If writing this card was so important, why did I forget about it for so long? Are you as stumped as I am? Anyway, Aunt Thelma, I hope you like your gift. Andrew Dice Clay is one of the funniest new comedians around and the VHS of *Adventures of Ford Fairlane* will leave you in stitches. Enjoy!

Sorry I didn't get anybody else anything. Like I said, the decade (or fortnight?) whizzed by so quick. Maybe you can all have a movie night and go over to Aunt Thelma's to see *Adventures of Ford Fairlane*.

MERRY CHRISTMAS!

Lester Brogran

Merry Christmas from a Sleep-Deprivation Study

S O, ME AND THE FELLAS OPTED IN on this cushy sleep-deprivation study. Our goal is to remain awake anywhere from ninety-six to one hundred sixty-eight hours. For that we will receive five hundred dollars, which ain't bad for sitting around and doing not much of nothing.

Hour 16

I think the people in the next room are having sex. Either that or they're sleeping restlessly and agreeing with each other a lot.

Hour 25

Fueled on pepperoni pizza we decided to use our down time to write holiday letters to all of you. I'm feeling a little punchy so can't really think of anything to tell you about my year so far, but here's a jingle I just made up off the top of my head about, you guessed it, pizza! Dude, check it out:

> *Pizza shmeetza!*
> *I love you!*
> *Because you're fun*
> *And easy to chew.* '
> *O! Pizza shmeetza!*
> *I love you!*

Hour 30

A bunch of us come up with a can't miss holiday reality series called *When Elves Attack*. Don't steal this concept. It is gold! Or what about *Pimp My Tree*? Double gold!

"Mary, I've lost Zu-Zu's petals!" "Merry Christmas, you old Bedford Falls Savings & Loan!"

Hour 36

Merry Christmas from a naked guy. I am writing this naked.

Not naked sexy. More like sitting on the john naked and writing this. I wish I had some Pringles.

Hour 42 and 45 seconds

We're talking politics. I made up my mind that Vice President Lon Chaney, Jr. guy is a flea on tick on a dog's ass.

Just so you know, when someone you barely know asks, "How you doing?" It's not appropriate to answer, "I'm hurting real, real bad, Buddy. What did you say your phone number was, again?"

Shit. I wish we had some tequila shooters. Can you mail some?

So sleepy.

Hour 60

That Christmas tree taunts me.

"Shut up! Shut up! Shut up!"

Oh my God! The tinsel burns my eyes.

Hour 61

Help me.

Hour 61 and 8 seconds

'Tis the Season of (For)Giving from Rock, Paper, Scissors

Dear Friends,

Seasons greetings from your friends, Rock, Paper, Scissors.

This is a tough letter to write, and not just because we are inanimate objects. All those years we said we were away on business during Christmas—who were we kidding? Now it's finally time to pay the piper, admit our gambling addiction, and maybe make amends to some of you. That's what the holidays are all about, right? Fresh starts and new beginnings, right?

Sure, it's been quite a ride. Quite a ride. For a while we were on top. Our footloose trio settled bar bets, playground brawls, and even went into space. We hung out with kings and queens, Joey Bishop who is one cool Vegas cat, and even those crazy bastards the French who insisted on calling us Rochambeau. We settled the Hatfield–McCoy Feud (despite what you heard) and toured with KISS. But things started to go crazy and spiral down around the time millions of kids clamored for the video game version of Rock, Paper, Scissors. Scissors overdid it with the Jack Daniels and got hurt running. While recuperating, he started thinking about how his life had gone. With as many women as we've partied with, I reckon we all got a pebble, Post-it, or pair of safety scissors stashed away somewhere. It's not enough to just send the kid a check once in a while or every few Christmasses.

In hindsight, after Scissors left the group, we didn't make some of the best choices. Rock, Paper, Flame Thrower was a big mistake, and Rock, Paper, Dynamite and Rock, Paper, and Rock, Paper, Hentai Manga were no better. Life has a way of hitting you right in the snot box, so it wasn't long before we hit (Rock) bottom. Arrested as an enemy combatant and taken to prison at Guantanamo Bay, Cuba, where we were forced to play Russian roulette against each other, like in *The Deer Hunter* was our wake-up call. Thank God for the ACLU. And thank scissors for rejoining the trio.

Some of us kinda feel like you got us into this mess. But that wouldn't be accepting responsibility for our actions, which is like, Step Seven. Saying sorry is never easy, but that's what we aim to do. We used to operate on the assumption that in a game of chance there are no wrong answers. Now, we know that's not true. Starting January 1 we promise to beat this gambling addiction. This includes Internet gambling, the stock market, commodities, options, buying or playing lottery tickets, raffle tickets, flipping a coin, entering the office sport pool, or even the game that is our namesake. Mark our words that from now on you will never hear the following:

✔ Rock breaks or blunts Scissors: Rock wins.

✔ Scissors cut Paper: Scissors wins.

✔ Paper covers Rock: Paper wins.

Don't tempt us. Don't invoke us. From now on, call Once, Twice, Three: Shoot or, better yet, don't do nothing.

God grant us the serenity.

SINCERELY YOURS,
Rock, Paper, Scissors

Take the Twelve Nights of Christmas Lunesta Challenge

ASK YOUR DOCTOR OR COLLEGE-AGE CHILD how to get twelve nights of Lunesta absolutely free!

How are you sleeping during these days? Do you have trouble falling asleep, worrying that, with so many relatives coming and going and staying over, some valuable possessions will go missing—or, worse, cousin Alice will stumble upon your secret stash of online porn in the computer file marked *tax notes*? Of course you do.

Maybe it's time to take the Twelve Nights of Christmas Lunesta challenge. See how it can help you find the full night's sleep you've been craving.

Hurry! Offer ends December 31!

Important Safety Information: Lunesta works quickly, and should be taken right before bed. It should not be taken before hanging Christmas lights, operating a snowplow, carving a turkey, assembling a bicycle, rearranging furniture, discussion of your spouses' needs, or attending a religious service. Be sure you have at least twelve hours to devote to sleep before becoming active. Do not use alcohol or Viagra while taking Lunesta. This will lead to misunderstandings and/or memory loss. Most sleep medicines carry some risk of dependency. Lunesta is designed to get you through a rough patch especially during the holidays, which, let's face it, ain't all they're cracked up to be. Side effects may include unpleasant taste, headache, drowsiness, and dizziness, which may be indistinguishable from your general holiday malaise.

CHRISTMAS INSTANT MESSAGING

\<Joo C> Hey, you know what sucks?

\<ICU2> Vacuums

\<Joo C> Hey, you know what sucks in a metaphorical sense?

\<ICU2> Black holes

\<Joo C> Hey, you know what just isn't cool?

\<ICU2> Lava?

\<Joo C> Hey, you know what hangs from my tree?

\<ICU2> Your xmas balls

\<Joo C> Hey, your holiday blog sucks

\<ICU2> I got your holiday blog right here, Pal.

Giving Holiday No Thanks, Hollywood Style

MY ASSISTANT IS WRITING YOU TO EXPRESS MY sincerest appreciation for your non-faith-specific holiday-giving efforts. Your submission of a hand-knit adult onesie was certainly a unique choice and an interesting project. I loved it. *Loved* it! However, I do have some concerns and feel that this item may not be quite right for me at this time. I know that you mentioned something about the onesie being a one-of-a-kind original, hand-knitted by your blind grandmother. Very sweet, but truthfully, *original* scares me a bit. I prefer items that are uniquely familiar. By chance, did Granny provide a gift receipt? If not, please know that the return of this gift in no way reflects on its merit or the quality of the knitting.

Best of luck with your future gift-giving endeavors.

REGARDS,

Brad Rosensweigfelder
ICA Pictures

Merry Christmas from Your Secret Santa

★ ★ ★ ★ ★

Dear Sarah Reynolds,

I ADMIT THAT MY GIFT OF USED RUBBER GLOVES WAS IN poor taste but, then again, I don't know you all that well except for what I was able to glean from hacking into your office e-mail after hours. Unlike you, I haven't been blessed with an active personal life. Just to weigh in, I do agree that giving Stephan's lack of interest in a long-term commitment is troublesome. Can you say Loser with a capital L? Just my opinion, but what you gave him during that long weekend in Toronto was the ultimate selfless act in a relationship, no matter how slutty it sounded to some of us around the water cooler. (That was certainly one way to wax the hood of a Cadillac! *-0)

As far as the gloves go . . . Let me just say that unlike your GNP-sized year-end bonus, mine barely managed a purchase from the vending machine downstairs. If you're getting six figures, I'm pulling down stick figures. So, after purchasing my Rock Star, I was caught short and pretty much had to raid the janitor's closet. (If you need one of those Swiffer mops, I now have three.) But, much like duct tape (or is it duck tape?), gloves can come in handy for all kinds of situations. Anyhow, don't get the wrong idea about my lack of Sacagaweas. Unlike some of the geek-o-palosers we have given tech support a bad rep, I'm proud to say that I no longer live at home. If you noticed that extra bounce in my step lately, it's because I scored a killer basement apartment. Some people are picky about living below sea level but not me. It's their loss, my gain. Right? I'm looking forward to when you pop by to check it out. I'll always have a plate of Christmas cookies on hand just in case.

Also, just so you know, I keep mistletoe under the desk in my cubicle. I'm pretty sure it's going to come in handy at the office Christmas party. I understand that things can get pret-tay freak-ay. If you want to wear the gloves, that will be our signal. Until then, feel free to check out either of my two blogs

at **www.brucechadleyflyingsolo.com**

or **www.allaboutsarahreynolds.com.**

I'm sure you'll appreciate the tributes. I kinda got carried away with some of them.

BEST,
Bruce Chadley,
Your Secret Santa

SEASONAL TIDINGS

from ~~101~~ Twenty-One Realistic Things to Do Before You Die

THE HOLIDAYS ARE A TIME FOR ENDINGS and beginnings, reflecting on the past and planting seeds for the future. As you start the new year, please accept this gift of ~~101~~ Twenty-One Realistic Things to Do Before You Die.

1. Pay for this book.

2. Bequeath this book to a loved one.

3. Clone yourself, so you can keep living.

4. Swim with a great white while wearing a bacon Speedo.

5. Win an award. If you've done nothing to warrant an award, treat yourself to a PhD from Phoenix University's online school. You deserve it.

6. Write a best-selling novel. If you don't have time for this, post a Yahoo video of yourself reading a best-selling novel while naked.

7. Be part of a threesome. Pets, sock puppets, or Dick Cheney do not count.

8. Learn to play "Free Bird" on the kazoo.

9. Catch a lightning bolt. Extra credit if you catch the bolt between your teeth. (Sitting on a roof top during an electrical storm while wearing a suit made of aluminum foil will help; however, biting into a power line is considered cheating.)

10. Heckle a Quaker meeting. (Self-explanatory.)

11. Finger a perp. (Note: This should be done in a police lineup and not in a public restroom.

12. Join the Mile High(way) Club. Sex on a Greyhound bus rambling along the interstate entails all the thrills you might expect. (Extra credit if the bus does **not** have a bathroom.)

13. Visit every rest stop in Teaneck, New Jersey. (Extra credit: Crawl out of the bushes with your pants around your ankles proclaiming, "Wow! That was some loving!") If rest areas are in short supply, strip clubs will do.

14. Get a tattoo that makes a real statement. Suggestions: "Born to die." "I love Satan!" "I support the war but not the troops." Years from now you'll be a big hit in the retirement home.

15. Buy top-of-the-line Nike running shoes, then watch a marathon from start to finish on television. Be sure to stay hydrated.

16. Join a cult. (Lethal Kool-Aid optional.)

17. Tell your children they're adopted even if they aren't.

18. Go to your local senior center to teach octogenarians the Kama Sutra.

19. Visit the Seven Blunders of the Modern World. (Pending completion of the George W. Bush Presidential Library that will house Nos. 3–7.)

20. Make love in a forest. (Partner preferable but optional.)

21. Memorize a poem, limerick, or sea shanty. Pass said limerick or sea shanty down to your heirs requesting that they recite it at your funeral. Some suggestions:

There was a Young Person of Smyrna
Whose grandmother threatened to burn her;
But she seized on the cat, and said, "Granny, burn that!
You incongruous old woman of Smyrna!"

AND

Shantyman: Boney was a worrier,
All: Way, hey, ya!
Shantyman: A worrier and disease carrier,
All: Jean-François!

Burning Man CHRISTMAS

BROTHER, THINGS CAN GET A LITTLE BUSY AROUND Christmas time, don't cha know? Here's everything you didn't hear about, yet.

Last year at this time, I was working in the nursing home. Remember we woke up all the oldsters to celebrate New Year's Eve? Only it was just a bit after nine o'clock, since most of them wouldn't make it to the real stroke of midnight. We thought it would be fun to ring in the new year but it ended up being a big mistake. At the countdown, they all took out their teeth and threw them in the air. Something like forty sets of teeth. We spent the next three days trying to match up the dentures. Damn. There's just no easy way to try out a big tray of teeth.

So, six months ago, me and Tim had had enough and we cashed in some old baseball cards my Dad had. We bought a Winnebago. I think it only had three wheels at the time. But it had style. Tim christened it the Wimminbago for obvious reasons.

We got the fourth wheel, put the hammer down, and headed west, young man to a chunk of change—120 miles north or so of Reno.

Let me just say that if you're going to walk around for five days with just one shoe tripped out on you name it Burning Man is *the* place to be. Even though the Wimminbago died ten miles from the camping area and we had to continue on foot and sleep in tents like the other squeabs, BM was the highlight of our year, maybe even our lives. This proto hippie apocalyptic freakfest is a mecca for pyromaniacs and art lovers. It's the one place where you can forgo bathing for a week and still hook up with someone covered in glitter and wearing a neon wig. And if things progress like they should, you'll be doing the deed with Miss Glitter in front of two hundred screaming squeabs. More than likely the night will end with the sunrise and a discussion of your significant others back home. As you know, neither Tim nor I have "others," but that didn't stop us from making some up. We bared our souls to the glitter girls, confided our deepest secrets. An hour later, I couldn't remember what any of them were. If wasn't for all the glitter all over my hands, I'd say I hallucinated the whole thing.

But Burning Man isn't just about the ritualistic torching of the large wooden man, random hookups, and eating food covered in dust and sand. It's something much deeper. We even write down wishes on pieces of paper and burn them with the large wooden dude himself.

During the day we melted like crayons in the 110 degree heat. At night we froze our asses off. But it wasn't just about survival. One righteous ultimate fightinglike spectacle, named *Thunderdome* after the *Mad Max* movie, uses elastic pulleys to swing people holding foam-wrapped weapons into each other to do battle. Stumbling around, it's like one mighty mass NEA grant.

Like I said, we did a lot of sex and drugs. A lot. Mostly other people's. We discovered that Burning Man knows you were invented to begin with. We changed our names to Flying Horse and Sir Chadwick.

"You can just be whatever it is you need to be, today." Of course, the pressure to find a new self upon arrival can take a serious psychic toll especially when you're coming down, grumpy, cold, and naked. We lived on Hamburger Helper.

Even as the tents are coming down, everybody's talking about *next year*. Mostly that means all the stuff you'll remember to bring and people you'll hook up with. It's rough going back to regular life like the nursing home with the bedpans and whatnot.

May the Burning Man spirit burn inside you this Christmas.

Stop by anytime.

PEACE,

Kirk Wilson

LAETA SATURNALIA!
from Pompeii

Planning just the right holiday destination doesn't have to be such a chore.

No matter what gods you worship, here in modern-day 79 A.D., the city of Pompeii really knows how to live! Nestled in the shade of pristine Mt. Vesuvius, Pompeii erupts with celebration during the holidays.

By Priapus and Jupiter, our bathhouse orgies and therapeutic ash body wraps are second to none!

Now, serving the popular eastern cults of Christianity and Isis!

Hotel amenities include your own personal shrine and slave in every room!

Blown glass!

Se habla Espanol!

Pornographic mosaics of your family commissioned on site! (Disproportionately large genitals guaranteed or you don't pay!)

Come to Pompeii, where the holidays sizzle!

Complimentary human sacrifice to please your personal deity!

🌲 Lettermatic 3000 Form Holiday Letter 🌲

Gosh, _____ has been quite a _____
year. I have to say that we've been particularly blessed with
the arrival of the _____. As _____ used
to say, "It's so true that it is _____
that matters most." We opened this year with a resolution
to_____. Our latest hobby is _____. It's
really a lot of fun.

_____ is still _____. _____
turns ____ this year. You'll be astonished to hear that _____
_____ turns ___ in _____. My, how time flies!

We hear that _____ has moved back home at the
age of ___. Here's hoping he/she finds himself/herself without
another stint in _____.

Enclosed are pictures from our big trip to _____.
We tried to stop in for a surprise visit to _____ but,
apparently, they weren't home.

My _____ has been acting up a bit, but otherwise I
can't complain. Our neighbor _____ has trouble with
his/her _____. Poor _____.

Here's hoping that _____ brings you wonderful things.

May the blessings of the season be upon you. Happy holidays from all of us.

LOVE,
The _____ Family.

Acknowledgments

SEVERAL PEOPLE ARE TO BLAME FOR THE EXISTENCE of this labor of levity. The boundless encouragement of my dear wife, Sonia, is a good place to start. Somehow, I still manage to make her laugh, usually at the wrong times, and soy milk out of her nose remains my Holy Grail. My dad and my grandparents all had good senses of humor. My grandma, Mary Lent, in particular, liked to laugh and, growing up, I delighted in seeing her blue eyes twinkle with mirth. They've all passed on now, yet, I have felt their presence keenly as I toiled on the page these past months.

Good writers need great editors. So-so writers need really, really great editors. That's a fact of life. I leave it to you, the reader, which category I fall into, but I will state this:

Amanda Patten is a really, really good editor.

Thanks to my agent Daniel Greenberg for his guidance.

Christmas Letters from Hell began life as a slim tome published in limited edition through the BookSurge division of Amazon Books. Thanks very much to my dear editor/designer Paula Johnson, who was responsible for the look and feel of that edition. It pays to have a force of nature on one's side and that is Paula.

Finally, no writer with toddlers in the house ever truly writes alone (or uses the bathroom or reads the Sunday paper or sleeps at 6:32 A.M. or . . .). Thanks to our son Willem and our daughter Sophia Skye for teaching their Daddy a thing or two about mixing humor with sleep deprivation.

Love those kids.